Atlas of the Maldives

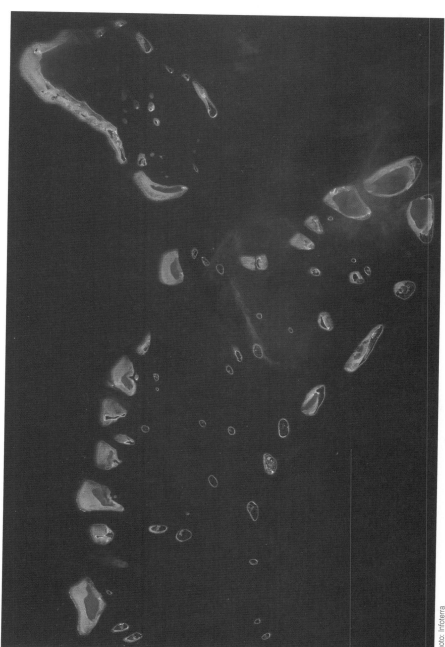

Photo: Infoterra

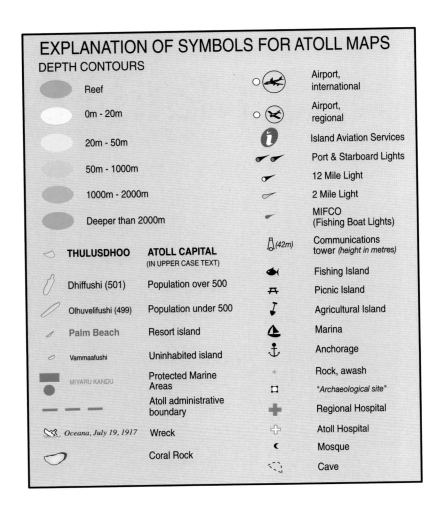

EXPLANATION OF SYMBOLS FOR ATOLL MAPS

DEPTH CONTOURS

- Reef
- 0m - 20m
- 20m - 50m
- 50m - 1000m
- 1000m - 2000m
- Deeper than 2000m

THULUSDHOO — ATOLL CAPITAL (IN UPPER CASE TEXT)

Dhiffushi (501) — Population over 500

Olhuvelifushi (499) — Population under 500

Palm Beach — Resort island

Vammaafushi — Uninhabited island

MIYARU KANDU — Protected Marine Areas

— Atoll administrative boundary

Oceana, July 19, 1917 — Wreck

Coral Rock

- Airport, international
- Airport, regional
- Island Aviation Services
- Port & Starboard Lights
- 12 Mile Light
- 2 Mile Light
- MIFCO (Fishing Boat Lights)
- (42m) Communications tower (height in metres)
- Fishing Island
- Picnic Island
- Agricultural Island
- Marina
- Anchorage
- Rock, awash
- "Archaeological site"
- Regional Hospital
- Atoll Hospital
- Mosque
- Cave

Atlas of the Maldives, 2004
ISBN 1 876410 42 6
Research and text by Tim Godfrey

Publisher: Atoll Editions, PO Box 113,
Apollo Bay, Victoria, 3233, Australia
Fax (+61) 3 52376332
Email: atolled@bigpond.com
Atoll Maps by Country Cartographics
Layout Design by Karen Rempel
Finished art by Munch Design

First Published as Malways,
Maldives Island Directory in 1996.
Second Edition 1998.
Third Edition 1999.

UPDATING charts is an ongoing task that relies greatly on the input of individuals as well as private businesses and government organizations. Sometimes a reef will be encountered that is not shown on a chart, or a new name will be given to an island or reef. Perhaps divers locate a wreck or a marked light is found to be in the wrong position. Changes are occurring all the time at an increasingly rapid rate and Atoll Editions is grateful to all those who have contributed in many ways to the production of this Atlas. We invite readers to notify us of any observations they feel should be included or changed in future editions of the Atlas.

Atoll Editions would like to acknowledge permission granted by the UK Hydrographic Office for the use of their Uligamu island chart. We are particularly grateful for the support of the Ministry of Transport & Civil Aviation, Ministry of Atolls Administration, Ministry of Construction & Public Works, Ministry of Tourism, Ministry of Agriculture & Fisheries, National Centre for Linguistic & Historical Research and the Hulhumalé Development Section. Also, to our sponsors Dhiraagu, Island Aviation Services and Maldivian Air Taxi.

Photos by Tim Godfrey, unless stated otherwise.
Cover Photo: Islands in Alifu Dhaalu with Hanghghaameedhoo in foreground.
Photo by Sigurd Schjoett
Back Cover Photo: Photo by Adrian Neville.

Atlas of the Maldives

Contents

DhiMobile

Coverage Map of Maldives

Haa Alifu Atoll

Dhidhdhoo

Haa Dhaalu Atoll

Kulhudhuffushi

Shaviyani Atoll

Funadhoo

Raa Atoll

Noonu Atoll

Ugoofaaru

Manadhoo

Naifaru

Lhaviyani Atoll

Baa Atoll

Eydhafushi

North Alifu Atoll

Rasdhoo

Thulusdhoo

Male'

Kaafu Atoll

Mahibadhoo

South Alifu Atoll

Felidhu

Vaavu Atoll

Faafu Atoll

Magoodhoo

Meemu Atoll

Mull

Dhaalu Atoll

Kudahuvadhoo

Thaa Atoll

Veymandoo

Laamu Atoll

Fonadhoo

Gaafu Alifu Atoll

Vilingili

Thinadhoo

Gaafu Dhaalu Atoll

Gnaviyani Atoll

Fua-Mulah

Hithadhoo

Seenu Atoll

N

- ● Indoor Coverage
- ● Marginal Indoor Coverage
- ● Outdoor Coverage (Sea Coverage)

DhiMobile coverage is available in ALL Resorts.

Coverage as at December 2003

DHIRAAGU
www.dhiraagu.com.mv

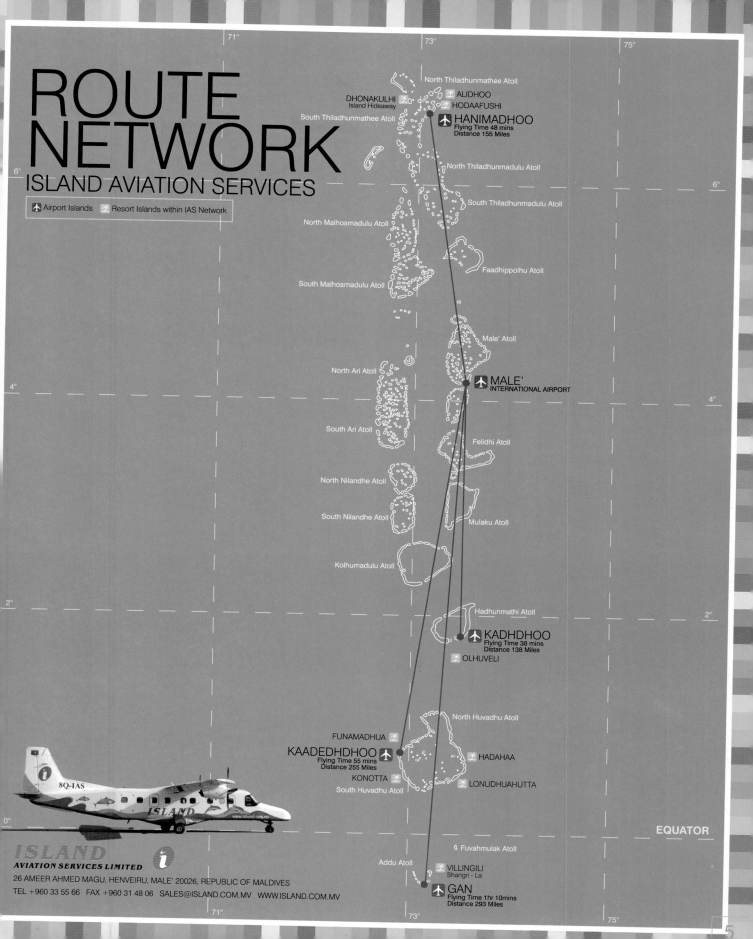

ROUTE NETWORK
ISLAND AVIATION SERVICES

✈ Airport Islands   🏝 Resort Islands within IAS Network

North Thiladhunmathee Atoll

DHONAKULHI
Island Hideaway

🏝 ALIDHOO
🏝 HODAAFUSHI

✈ **HANIMADHOO**
Flying Time 48 mins
Distance 155 Miles

South Thiladhunmathee Atoll

North Thiladhunmadulu Atoll

South Thiladhunmadulu Atoll

North Malhosmadulu Atoll

Faadhippolhu Atoll

South Malhosmadulu Atoll

Male' Atoll

North Ari Atoll

✈ **MALE'**
INTERNATIONAL AIRPORT

South Ari Atoll

Felidhi Atoll

North Nilandhe Atoll

South Nilandhe Atoll

Mulaku Atoll

Kolhumadulu Atoll

Hadhunmathi Atoll

✈ **KADHDHOO**
Flying Time 38 mins
Distance 138 Miles

🏝 OLHUVELI

North Huvadhu Atoll

FUNAMADHUA 🏝

KAADEDHDHOO ✈
Flying Time 55 mins
Distance 255 Miles

🏝 HADAHAA

KONOTTA 🏝
South Huvadhu Atoll

🏝 LONUDHUAHUTTA

EQUATOR

Fuvahmulak Atoll

Addu Atoll

🏝 VILLINGILI
Shangri - La

✈ **GAN**
Flying Time 1hr 10mins
Distance 293 Miles

8Q-IAS   ISLAND   www.island.com.mv

ISLAND
AVIATION SERVICES LIMITED
26 AMEER AHMED MAGU, HENVEIRU, MALE' 20026, REPUBLIC OF MALDIVES
TEL +960 33 55 66   FAX +960 31 48 06   SALES@ISLAND.COM.MV   WWW.ISLAND.COM.MV

6°   6°
4°   4°
2°   2°
0°
71°   73°   75°

5

"Dictionary"

air taxi / ear taeksi / noun (C) short form for Maldivian Air Taxi, an airline in the Maldives operating Twin Otter seaplanes, in the business of transferring tourists to and from their resort destinations; *Air Taxi maintains an uncompromising level of safety · The staff at Air Taxi are friendly and professional · In operation since 1993, Air Taxi is reliable, dependable operator in the Maldives.*

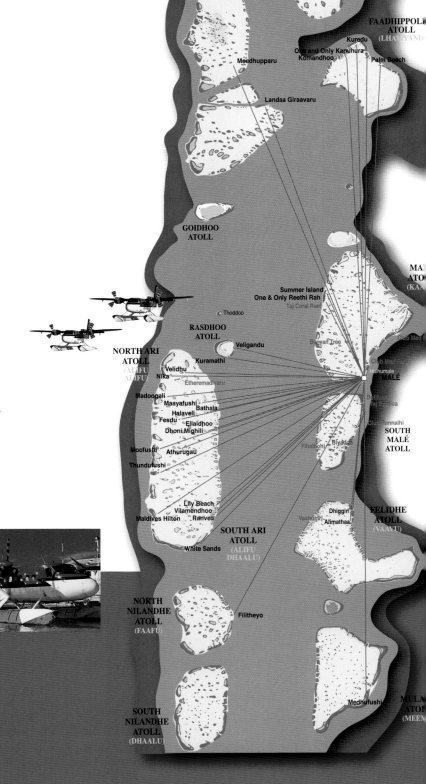

MALDIVIAN AIR TAXI

Maldivian Air Taxi (Pte.) Ltd. – P.O. Box 2023 Male' Republic of Maldives – Phone: (+960) 31 52 01 – Fax: (+960) 31 52 03 – mail:mat@mat.com.m – www.mataxi.com

Cado Graphic Design

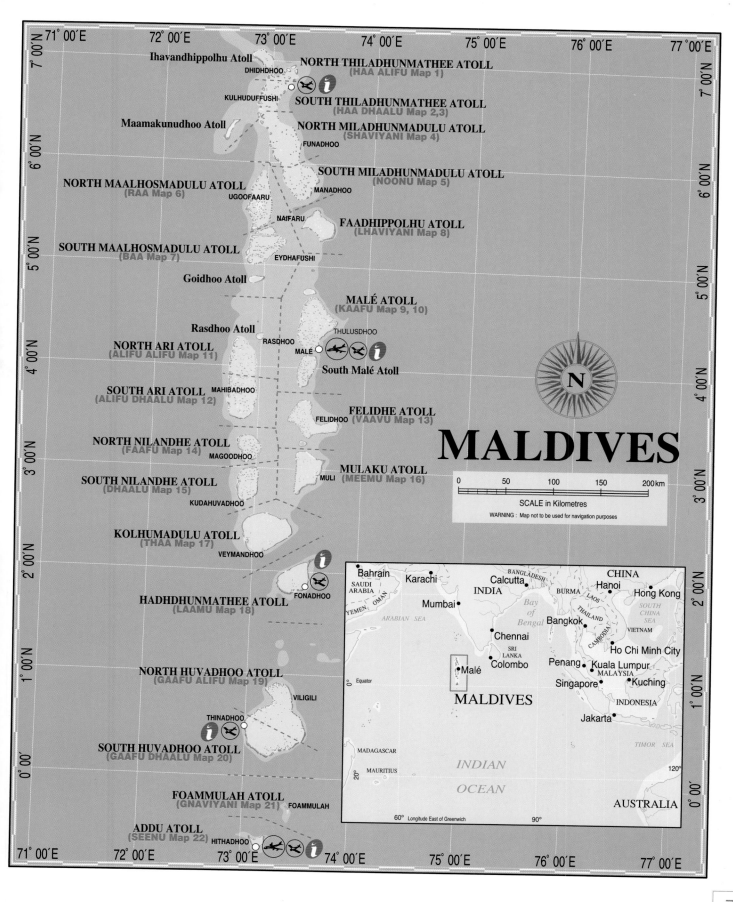

MALDIVES

Ihavandhippolhu Atoll

NORTH THILADHUNMATHEE ATOLL
(HAA ALIFU Map 1)

DHIDHDHOO

KULHUDUFFUSHI

SOUTH THILADHUNMATHEE ATOLL
(HAA DHAALU Map 2,3)

Maamakunudhoo Atoll

NORTH MILADHUNMADULU ATOLL
(SHAVIYANI Map 4)

FUNADHOO

SOUTH MILADHUNMADULU ATOLL
(NOONU Map 5)

NORTH MAALHOSMADULU ATOLL
(RAA Map 6)

UGOOFAARU

MANADHOO

NAIFARU

FAADHIPPOLHU ATOLL
(LHAVIYANI Map 8)

SOUTH MAALHOSMADULU ATOLL
(BAA Map 7)

EYDHAFUSHI

Goidhoo Atoll

MALÉ ATOLL
(KAAFU Map 9, 10)

Rasdhoo Atoll

THULUSDHOO

RASDHOO

MALÉ

NORTH ARI ATOLL
(ALIFU ALIFU Map 11)

South Malé Atoll

SOUTH ARI ATOLL
(ALIFU DHAALU Map 12)

MAHIBADHOO

FELIDHE ATOLL
(VAAVU Map 13)

FELIDHOO

NORTH NILANDHE ATOLL
(FAAFU Map 14)

MAGOODHOO

MULAKU ATOLL
(MEEMU Map 16)

MULI

SOUTH NILANDHE ATOLL
(DHAALU Map 15)

KUDAHUVADHOO

KOLHUMADULU ATOLL
(THAA Map 17)

VEYMANDHOO

FONADHOO

HADHDHUNMATHEE ATOLL
(LAAMU Map 18)

NORTH HUVADHOO ATOLL
(GAAFU ALIFU Map 19)

VILIGILI

THINADHOO

SOUTH HUVADHOO ATOLL
(GAAFU DHAALU Map 20)

FOAMMULAH ATOLL
(GNAVIYANI Map 21)

FOAMMULAH

ADDU ATOLL
(SEENU Map 22)

HITHADHOO

| 0 | 50 | 100 | 150 | 200km |

SCALE in Kilometres

WARNING : Map not to be used for navigation purposes

Bahrain

Karachi

Calcutta

CHINA

Hanoi

Hong Kong

SAUDI ARABIA

YEMEN

OMAN

INDIA

BANGLADESH

BURMA

LAOS

THAILAND

VIETNAM

Mumbai

ARABIAN SEA

Bay of Bengal

Bangkok

CAMBODIA

SOUTH CHINA SEA

Chennai

SRI LANKA

Ho Chi Minh City

Colombo

Penang

Kuala Lumpur

MALAYSIA

Kuching

Malé

Singapore

INDONESIA

0° Equator

MALDIVES

Jakarta

MADAGASCAR

20°

MAURITIUS

INDIAN OCEAN

TIMOR SEA

120°

AUSTRALIA

60° Longitude East of Greenwich

90°

Atlas of the Maldives
Introduction

The marvellous and once mysterious Maldive Islands, remain just as intriguing as ever and continue to divulge their secrets with every passing year. Atlas of the Maldives illustrates the diversity of geographical, historical and cultural features that make up this Indian Ocean Archipelago, as well as making island identification and location easier. It includes underwater maps of Protected Marine Areas as well as navigation lights, shipwrecks, and a comprehensive island index.

As the resorts continue to expand into the outer atolls, they provide the basis for change, bringing added interest to the regions they serve. The atoll charts include resorts and the location of proposed resorts. In recognising the importance of island names to the history of the Maldives, traditional island names are included in brackets when a resort changes the island's name.

New harbours and reclamation of land are constantly changing the shape of islands. Some maps of key islands have been included, revealing in considerable detail, some of these changes. When complemented with photos, Atlas of the Maldives illustrates the lifestyle, development aspirations and resources of the people.

Most importantly, this atlas is designed to be an informative reference for travelling around the atolls. Having a clear understanding of the island names and their locations, as well as knowing some of the main features, will undoubtedly lead to a more rewarding travel experience.

ATOLLS OF THE MALDIVES

In the English dictionary, an 'atoll' is defined as "a ring-shaped coral reef and small island, enclosing a lagoon and surrounded by open sea." Within this definition, there are many hundreds of atolls in the Maldives. In broader terms these 'micro' atolls make up 25 distinct geographical atoll formations. They are spread in a north – south direction over a distance of 868 km between latitude 7°6'30"N and 0°42'30"S.

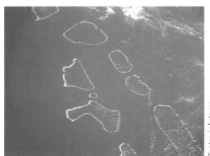

Satellite image of the central atolls of the Maldives.

Photo: infoterra

The British Admiralty, in their comprehensive bathymetric survey of the islands in 1834-36, defined where these atoll boundaries were and named each atoll according to local names. Open seas or deep channels with a depth of more than 200 metres separate the 25 atolls. If Kuda Kanduolhi - a 200 metre deep channel that divides South Maalhosmadulu Atoll - is considered an atoll division, then the total number of atolls is 26. The largest atoll, Huvadhoo, is 65 km wide and 82 km long, while Thoddoo, the smallest, is about 1.8 km in diameter. Depths within the atolls usually vary between 30 to 50 metres but in some places, such as Huvadhoo Atoll, depths may reach up to 90 metres.

The word "atoll" is derived from the Maldivian word "atholu", the only Maldivian word to have found it's way into the English dictionary. An atholu is an administrative region that in some parts of the Maldives, takes in more or less of these distinctly separate geographical coral reef formations. From the viewpoint of a boatman, sailing the length of the Maldives, most of the islands in the south are clearly part of distinctly separate atolls. In the north, however, many islands appear more isolated and the atoll boundaries appear less defined.

ADMINISTRATIVE REGIONS

The 25 atolls are divided into 21 administrative regions. Malé, the capital, is an entity in itself and makes up the 21st region. These administrative regions are named after the letters of the Maldivian alphabet and begin with "Haa", in the north to "Seenu", in the south. Some administrative regions are divided into north (alifu)/south (dhaalu) zones.

With so many islands in the Maldives- many with the same name- islands are usually identified by adding a prefix to the island name with the abbreviated letters of the Administrative region in which it lies. For instance, there are two islands with the name Govvaafushi.

HA Govvaafushi is in Haa Alifu while LH Govvaafushi is in Lhaviyani. Abbreviations for the regions are as follows: HA for Haa Alifu, HD for Haa Dhaalu, SH for Shaviyani, N for Noonu, RA for Raa, BA for Baa, LH for Lhaviyani, KA for Kaafu, AA for Alifu Alifu, AD for Alifu Dhaalu, FA for Faafu, DH for Dhaalu, ME for Meemu, TH for Thaa, LA for Laamu, GA for Gaafu Alifu, VA for Vaavu, GD for Gaafu Dhaalu, GN for Gnaviyani and SE for Seenu.

ISLANDS OF THE MALDIVES

There are an estimated 1190 islands in the Maldives with some form of vegetation on them, whether grass, bushes, or trees. Of this total, there are 200 inhabited islands and 990 uninhabited. This total figure can change from year to year as islands are continually being eroded and washed away, while others are being formed. Some islands, such as Thilafushi and Hulhumalé have been reclaimed. At a height of three metres, Hulhumalé is considered to be the highest island in the Maldives.

The number of 'inhabited' islands does not refer to the actual number of islands, but the administrative areas of those islands. For instance, Malé, the capital of the Maldives, includes Villingili and Hulhulmalé within it's administrative boundaries and all three are considered as 'one' island. In Seenu, Maradhoo and Maradhoo-Feydhoo are on the same geographical island but are considered as two separate 'islands'. The same applies to Meedhoo and Hulhudhoo, which have separate populations, but are on the same island. Other islands, like GD Fares and GD Maathoda have been joined together by land reclamation, but are still considered as separate islands.

Even though many uninhabited islands are unoccupied and in a natural state, many have some type of industry, whether it be agricultural or storage, and are clearly occupied at certain times, if not all the time. Tourist resorts are also defined as being 'uninhabited'.

POPULATION

The island population figures shown on the atoll maps are the registered populations of the islands based on the June 2003 survey. They are not based on the latest census figures. Census figures show the total population on an island at any given time and are not an accurate reflection of that island's permanent population. The total population of the Maldives in 2003 was 327,135.

Some islands are in the process of change. For instance, on SH Maakadoodhoo, (pop 1166) the entire population is being moved to SH Milandhoo, about 6kms to the north, because the current island does not offer a good harbour. About half the population has been moved, and when the transition is complete in a couple of year's time, SH Maakadoodhoo will become uninhabited. In the mean time, the registered population figures show SH Maakadoodhoo as being the inhabited island.

TOURISM

The Maldives has a yearly temperature range from 25° C to 32°C and two monsoon seasons, the NE Monsoon from December to April and the SW Monsoon, from May to November. The warm, tropical climate attracts divers and travellers from around the world to 88 resorts and 84 safari vessels, as well as guest houses and hotels in Malé, Hulhule and Gan. At the time of printing, four new resorts were under construction. In the north at Haa Alifu, Dhonakulhi (Island Hideaway) is proposed to be a resort marina, catering for the travelling yachtsmen. In Lhaviyani, Hudhufushi and in Baa, Landaa Giraavaru (Four Seasons Resort) are still under construction. In the south at Seenu, Villingili will open up the southern region with the International airport at Gan serving as the regions hub. In the next couple of years, a further 11 resorts are to be constructed throughout the remaining atolls of the Maldives, opening up the once isolated atolls for tourism.

NAVIGATION

The charts contained within this book are not designed for navigation and should not be used for such purposes. The latest British Admiralty surveys in WGS 84 datum, have been corrected for use with the Global Positioning System (GPS) and can be used in either chart or digital formats. However, the charts in this book can be used as an aid to navigation. They were compiled by using a combination of US satellite charts from 1986, British Admiralty Charts, black and white aerial transect survey photos from the 1960's and local knowledge from underwater diving surveys. Other features from various government departments and private organizations have been added to complement the charts.

The most useful visual reference while travelling around by boat are the Dhiraagu communication towers. There are 53 of them and they should all have a light at the top of the tower, making them visible at night. Towers less than 67m have a light at the top only. Tower heights exceeding that have a light at an intermediate height of

The island of Rasfari, Kaafu, showing its communication tower, one of 53 scattered around the atolls.

45m. At Foammulah, tower lights are at 3 different stages (45m, 90m & 120m). The tower at GD Gadhdhoo is of the same height and has lights at similar heights. In 2002 and 2003, 14 new towers 45M in height were erected within the atolls, these have been included on the charts.

LIGHTS

Since the year 2000, a program to establish navigation/marker lights in the atolls has been carried out by the Ministry of Transport & Civil Aviation. This major project involves identifying reefs, installing lights and marking their positions to enable safer, nighttime navigation for local vessels. For the first time, these lights are shown on Maldives charts. There are 85 lights with a 12-mile radius that have been constructed around the perimeter of the atolls and at the entrance to major shipping channels. A further 146 lights with a 2 mile radius have been established within the atolls to identify prominent reefs along the major trading routes. Along with the lights, an extra 63 reefs and channel names were added to the charts, bringing new identity to otherwise unnamed areas. The positions of all lights have been checked with the Ministry of Transport and Civil Aviation, however,

A 12 Mile Light, Velassaru Faru. Kaafu

caution should be exercised in relying on them. The 2 mile lights are designed for use by local boat captains only and new lights are constantly being added, some may be temporarily disabled, and others may even be moved. In addition, a further 30 MIFCO (Maldives Industrial Fisheries Company Ltd) lights have been included on the major trading routes in Huvadhoo Atoll.

REGIONAL DEVELOPMENT ISLANDS

A number of islands are being developed to provide all public conveniences and to act as hubs for island population growth. Facilities such as schools, hospitals and harbours are being directed to these islands as well as other investments to encourage employment. Land reclamation on some islands will provide more space for housing. These islands include HD Kulhudhuffushi, LH Naifaru, LA Fonadhoo-Gan, GN Foammulah, SE Hithadhoo.

FISHING ISLANDS

Fishing has traditionally been carried out by every inhabited island of the Maldives, but as the commercial industry has grown, so too have certain islands become hubs for the expanding fleets of vessels. There are 54 major fishing islands throughout the Maldives. They have been identified by the amount of fish-mainly tuna-caught over a three-year period from the year 2000. Employment at these islands is mostly based around fishing. From this total, a further 20 islands are identified as the major fish catching islands in the Maldives. These islands have been shown on the charts. There are currently four fishing zones within the Maldives. Each zone has two fishing operators that are based at different island ports. These islands include facilities for storing fish, whether they are frozen, chilled or live. The operators send collector vessels to outlying islands in their zone that specialise in catching and landing fish.

There are currently three fish processing islands in the Maldives. LH Felivaru has a fish canning factory and GA Kooddoo and LA Mundoo are cold storage and fish processing plants. A further three cold storage and fish processing plants are proposed for HA Huvahandhoo, SH Keekimini and TH Fonaddoo. KA Kanduoiygiri is a fresh chilled plant for processing larger fish like Yellow fin tuna into steaks.

FADS

There are currently 43 FADS (Fish Aggregating Devices) located in deep water around the outside of the Maldives.

They mostly occur between 12 to 15 nautical miles off the coast and are fastened with mooring lines to concrete blocks at about 3000 to 4000 metres. There position, however, is not always fixed. It varies with a radius of about one kilometre as the buoy swings on its axis. Buoys are sometimes cut or lost in heavy seas and replaced by another buoy in a different position. Also, fishermen sometimes request that the buoy be moved to other areas. For this reason, their positions have not been included on the charts. Fish, in particular tuna, are attracted to these floating devices and fishermen use them for pole and line fishing. The FADS are distributed evenly around every atoll. There are two types and those with lights and antennas are located at the extremities of the atolls as indicators to shipping.

AGRICULTURAL ISLANDS

Some inhabited and uninhabited islands are recognised as being major contributors to agricultural production in the Maldives. Some islands specialize in a particular fruit, vegetable or crop. AA Thoddoo, for instance, specializes in watermelons and chillies, SH Feevah in bananas and mango, HA Kelaa in vegetables like tomatoes and beans, as well as fruits such as banana and papaya, HD Vaikaradhoo in cereals like millet and sorghum, GD Vaadhoo and GN Gnaviyani in yams and taro, HD Finey in pumpkins and luffa, and KA Kaashidhoo in coconuts, chillies and bananas. SH Goidhoo is more general while GA Nilandhoo is more seasonal and tends to produce crops when the fishing is not as good, for instance in the SW Monsoon months of June and July, or before Ramadan. Other islands such as HD Nolhivaramu and ME Kolhuvaariyaafushi have only recently, in the past five years or so, become more productive in various cash crops. Other major producing islands such as LA Isdhoo, LA Kalaidhoo and GD Hoadedhdhoo, provide much of the produce for their atolls. GD Hoadedhdhoo even has a daily ferry to the capital Thinadhoo.

SHIPWRECKS

The Maldives Archipelago lies across the direct sea route between Southern Arabia, Sri Lanka and the Far East and was once a formidable barrier to shipping in the region. Many ships have run aground and remain on the reefs, often unidentified. Others are reported to have been wrecked but cannot be located. Some have been scuttled. A list of shipwrecks compiled by the Centre for Linguistic and Historical Research and other wrecks - located and reported by divers - are shown on the reefs where found. When a wreck is known to exist on a reef but has not been

The anchor from the Dutch East Indiaman Ravestein. Alifu Alifu.

Photo: Federico Fiorillo

identified, it often takes on the name of the reef on which it lies. Other ships known to have been wrecked but cannot be located, are included on the charts with their name and date (when known) positioned OFF the reef in the general area they were reported lost. G.P.S. positions of all wrecks are approximate positions, and are for reference only.

PROTECTED MARINE AREAS

On World Environment Day, June 5, 1995, the Government of the Maldives announced the establishment of 15 Protected Marine Areas within the major tourist atolls. A further nine areas were identified in 1999. These locations are shown on the charts and detailed underwater maps of these sites have been included. They are areas recognized for their diversity, significance or proximity to resorts and are exceptional diving areas. For these sites to be effectively protected, they need recognition and policing against marauding fishermen.

The island of Guraidhoo, Kaafu and Guraidhoo Kandu, a Protected Marine Area.

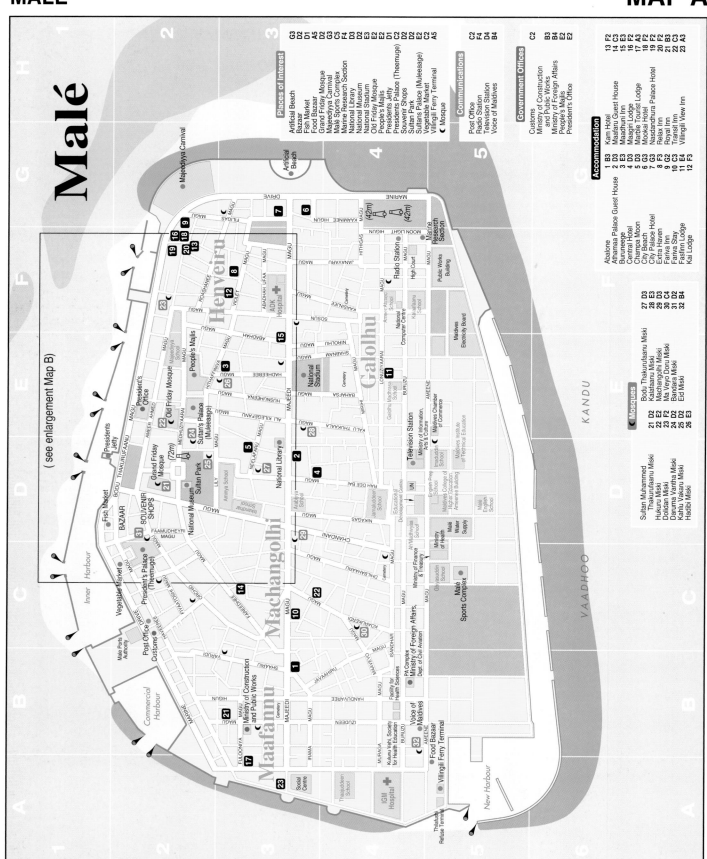

Satellite image of Malé taken December 2003.
Photo by SpaceImaging

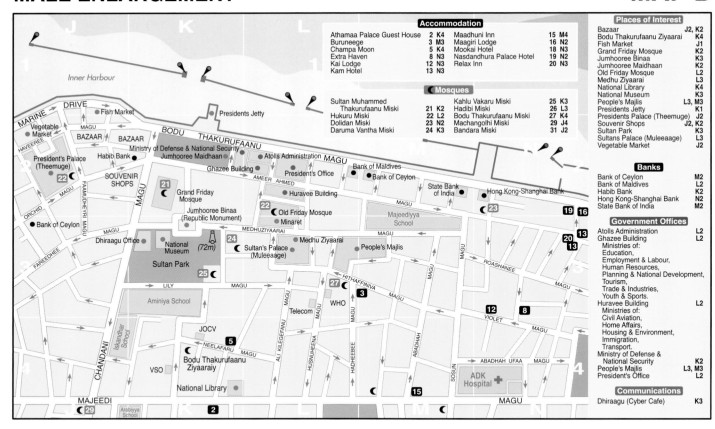

Accommodation

Athamaa Palace Guest House	2	K4
Buruneege	3	M3
Champa Moon	5	K4
Extra Haven	8	N3
Kai Lodge	12	N3
Kam Hotel	13	N3
Maadhuni Inn	15	M4
Maagiri Lodge	16	N2
Mookai Hotel	18	N3
Nasdandhura Palace Hotel	19	N2
Relax Inn	20	N3

Mosques

Sultan Muhammed Thakurufaanu Miski	21	K2
Hukuru Miski	22	L2
Dolidan Miski	23	N2
Daruma Vantha Miski	24	K3
Kahlu Vakaru Miski	25	K3
Hadibi Miski	26	L3
Bodu Thakurufaanu Miski	27	K4
Machangolhi Miski	29	J4
Bandara Miski	31	J2

Places of Interest

Bazaar	J2, K2
Bodu Thakurufaanu Ziyaarai	K4
Fish Market	J1
Grand Friday Mosque	K2
Jumhooree Binaa	K3
Jumhooree Maidhaan	K2
Old Friday Mosque	L2
Medhu Ziyaarai	L3
National Library	K4
National Museum	K3
People's Majlis	L3, M3
Presidents Jetty	K1
Presidents Palace (Theemuge)	J2
Souvenir Shops	J2, K2
Sultan Park	K3
Sultans Palace (Muleeaage)	L3
Vegetable Market	J2

Banks

Bank of Ceylon	M2
Bank of Maldives	L2
Habib Bank	K2
Hong Kong-Shanghai Bank	N2
State Bank of India	M2

Government Offices

Atolls Administration	L2
Ghazee Building	L2
Ministries of: Education, Employment & Labour, Human Resources, Planning & National Development, Tourism, Trade & Industries, Youth & Sports.	
Huravee Building	L2
Ministries of: Civil Aviation, Home Affairs, Housing & Environment, Immigration, Transport.	
Ministry of Defense & National Security	K2
People's Majlis	L3, M3
President's Office	L2

Communications

Dhiraagu (Cyber Cafe)	K3

MAP C

VILLINGILI

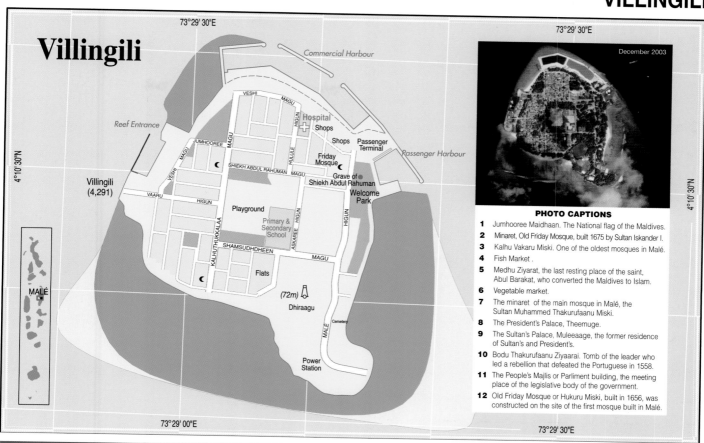

Villingili

Commercial Harbour

Reef Entrance

Villingili
(4,291)

MALÉ

VESHI MAGU
JUMHOOREE MAGU
VESHI
VAARU MAGU
HIGUN
SHIEKH ABDUL RAHUMAN MAGU
KALHUTHUKKALAA
SHAMSUDHDHEEN
MAGU
HIGUN
ASKAREE HIGUN
HIGUN
HULULE
Hospital
Shops
Shops
Passenger Terminal
Friday Mosque
Grave of Shiekh Abdul Rahuman
Welcome Park
Playground
Primary & Secondary School
Flats
(72m)
Dhiraagu
Cemetery
MALÉ
Power Station

Passenger Harbour

December 2003

PHOTO CAPTIONS

1. Jumhooree Maidhaan. The National flag of the Maldives.
2. Minaret, Old Friday Mosque, built 1675 by Sultan Iskander I.
3. Kalhu Vakaru Miski. One of the oldest mosques in Malé.
4. Fish Market .
5. Medhu Ziyarat, the last resting place of the saint, Abul Barakat, who converted the Maldives to Islam.
6. Vegetable market.
7. The minaret of the main mosque in Malé, the Sultan Muhammed Thakurufaanu Miski.
8. The President's Palace, Theemuge.
9. The Sultan's Palace, Muleeaage, the former residence of Sultan's and President's.
10. Bodu Thakurufaanu Ziyaarai. Tomb of the leader who led a rebellion that defeated the Portuguese in 1558.
11. The People's Majlis or Parliment building, the meeting place of the legislative body of the government.
12. Old Friday Mosque or Hukuru Miski, built in 1656, was constructed on the site of the first mosque built in Malé.

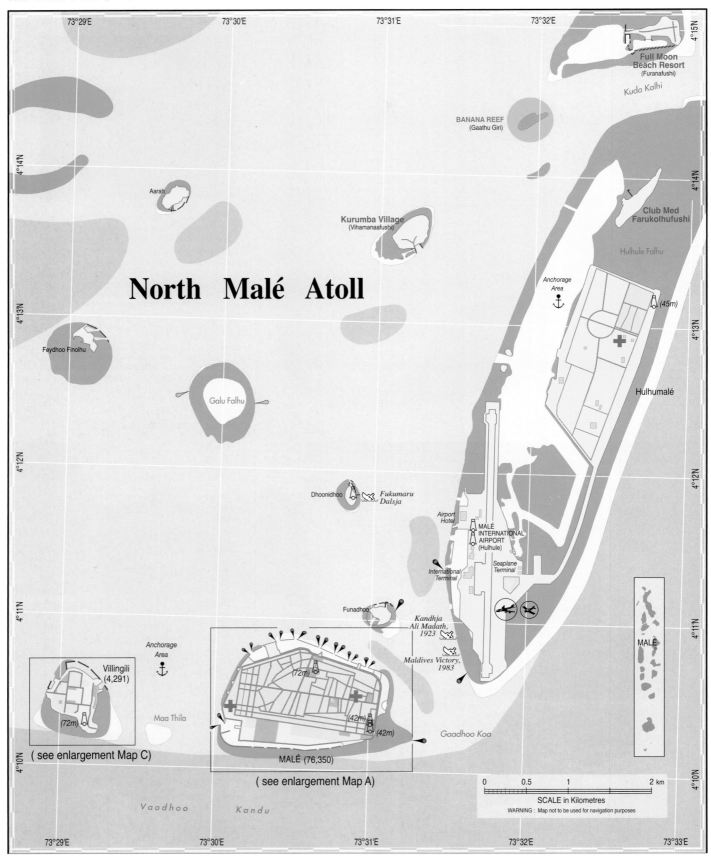

North Malé Atoll

Full Moon
Beach Resort
(Furanafushi)

Kuda Kalhi

BANANA REEF
(Gaathu Giri)

Aarah

Kurumba Village
(Vihamanaafushi)

Club Med
Farukolhufushi

Hulhule Falhu

Anchorage
Area

(45m)

Feydhoo Finolhu

Galu Falhu

Hulhumalé

Dhoonidhoo

Fukumaru
Dalsja

Airport
Hotel

MALÉ
INTERNATIONAL
AIRPORT
(Hulhule)

International
Terminal

Seaplane
Terminal

Funadhoo

Kandhja
Ali Madath,
1923

Maldives Victory,
1983

MALÉ

Anchorage
Area

Villingili
(4,291)

(72m)

(72m)

(42m)

(42m)

Maa Thila

MALÉ (76,350)

Gaadhoo Koa

(see enlargement Map C)

(see enlargement Map A)

Vaadhoo   Kandu

| 0 | 0.5 | 1 | 2 km |

SCALE in Kilometres

WARNING : Map not to be used for navigation purposes

Satellite Image of Malé and Hulhule area, December 2003.
Photo by SpaceImaging.

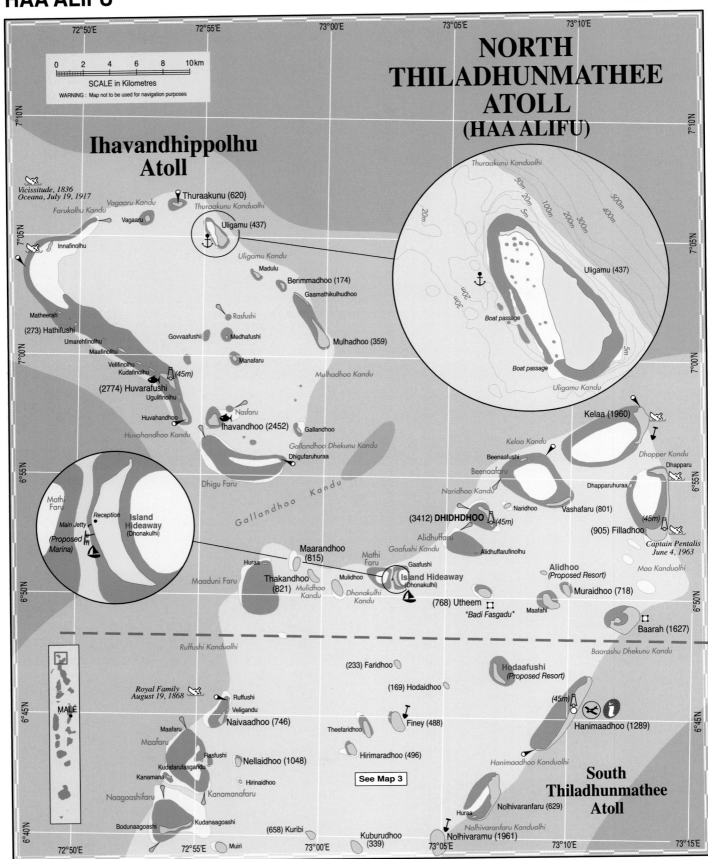

NORTH THILADHUNMATHEE ATOLL (HAA ALIFU)

Ihavandhippolhu Atoll

SCALE in Kilometres

0 2 4 6 8 10km

WARNING : Map not to be used for navigation purposes

Vicissitude, 1836
Oceana, July 19, 1917

Vagaaru Kandu

Farukolhu Kandu

Vagaaru

Innafinolhu

Thuraakunu (620)

Thuraakunu Kanduolhi

Uligamu (437)

Madulu

Berimmadhoo (174)

Gaamathikulhudhoo

Uligamu Kandu

Rasfushi

Matheerah

(273) Hathifushi

Umarehfinolhu

Maafinolhu

Govvaafushi

Medhafushi

Velifinolhu

Kudafinolhu *(45m)*

Manafaru

Mulhadhoo (359)

(2774) Huvarafushi

Ugulifinolhu

Huvahandhoo

Nasfaru

Huvahandhoo Kandu

Ihavandhoo (2452)

Gallandhoo

Mulhadhoo Kandu

Gallandhoo Dhekunu Kandu

Dhigufaruhuraa

Thuraakunu Kanduolhi

50m 20m 100m 200m 300m 400m 500m

20m

5m

Uligamu (437)

Boat passage

30m 20m

Boat passage

5m

Uligamu Kandu

Kelaa (1960)

Dhapper Kandu

Dhapparu

Beenaafushi

Beenaafaru

Dhapparuhuraa

Kelaa Kandu

Naridhoo

Vashafaru (801)

(45m)

(905) Filladhoo

Naridhoo Kandu

(3412) **DHIDHDHOO** *(45m)*

Alidhuffaru

Captain Pentalis
June 4, 1963

Alidhuffarufinolhu

Alidhoo
(Proposed Resort)

Muraidhoo (718)

Maa Kanduolhi

Dhigu Faru

Gallandhoo Kandu

Mathi Faru

Island Hideaway (Dhonakulhi)

Mathi Faru

Reception

Main Jetty

(Proposed Marina)

Maarandhoo (815)

Gaafushi Kandu

Gaafushi

Island Hideaway (Dhonakulhi)

Huraa

Thakandhoo (821)

Mulidhoo

Mulidhoo Kandu

Dhonakulhi Kandu

(768) Utheem
"Badi Fasgadu"

Maafahi

Baarah (1627)

Maaduni Faru

Ruffushi Kanduolhi

Baarashu Dhekunu Kandu

(233) Faridhoo

Hodaafushi
(Proposed Resort)

(169) Hodaidhoo

Royal Family
August 19, 1868

Ruffushi

Veligandu

Naivaadhoo (746)

Theefaridhoo

Finey (488)

(45m)

MALÉ

Maafaru

Maafaru

Rasfushi

Nellaidhoo (1048)

Hirimaradhoo (496)

Hanimaadhoo (1289)

Kudafarufasgandu

Hirinaidhoo

Kanamana

See Map 3

Kanamanafaru

Hanimaadhoo Kanduolhi

South Thiladhunmathee Atoll

Naagoashifaru

Bodunaagoashi

Kudanaagoashi

(658) Kuribi

Kuburudhoo (339)

Huraa

Nolhivaranfaru (629)

Nolhivaranfaru Kanduolhi

Nolhivaramu (1961)

Muiri

MAP 2

HAA DHAALU

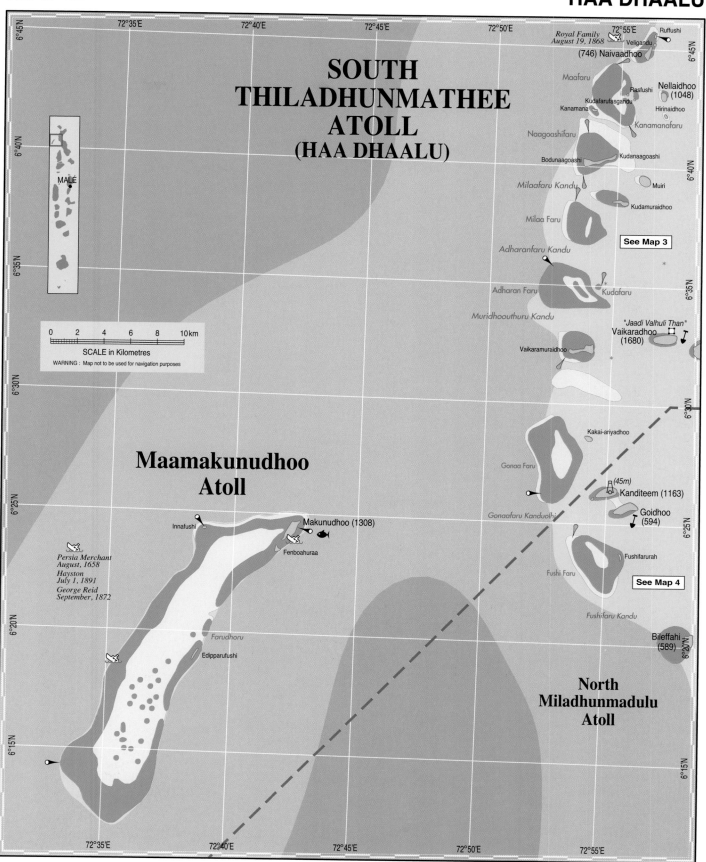

SOUTH THILADHUNMATHEE ATOLL (HAA DHAALU)

Royal Family
August 19, 1868

Ruffushi

Veligandu

(746) Naivaadhoo

Maafaru

Rasfushi

Nellaidhoo
(1048)

Kudafarufasgandu

Kanamana

Hirinaidhoo

Kanamanafaru

Naagoashifaru

Bodunaagoashi

Kudanaagoashi

Muiri

Milaafaru Kandu

Kudamuraidhoo

Milaa Faru

See Map 3

Adharanfaru Kandu

Adharan Faru

Kudafaru

"Jaadi Valhuli Than"

Muridhoouthuru Kandu

Vaikaradhoo
(1680)

Vaikaramuraidhoo

Maamakunudhoo
Atoll

Kakai-ariyadhoo

Gonaa Faru

(45m)

Kanditeem (1163)

Gonaafaru Kanduolhi

Goidhoo
(594)

Innafushi

Makunudhoo (1308)

Fenboahuraa

Fushifarurah

Persia Merchant
August, 1658
Hayston
July 1, 1891
George Reid
September, 1872

Fushi Faru

See Map 4

Fushifaru Kandu

Farudhoru

Bileffahi
(589)

Edipparufushi

North
Miladhunmadulu
Atoll

MALÉ

0 2 4 6 8 10km

SCALE in Kilometres

WARNING : Map not to be used for navigation purposes

19

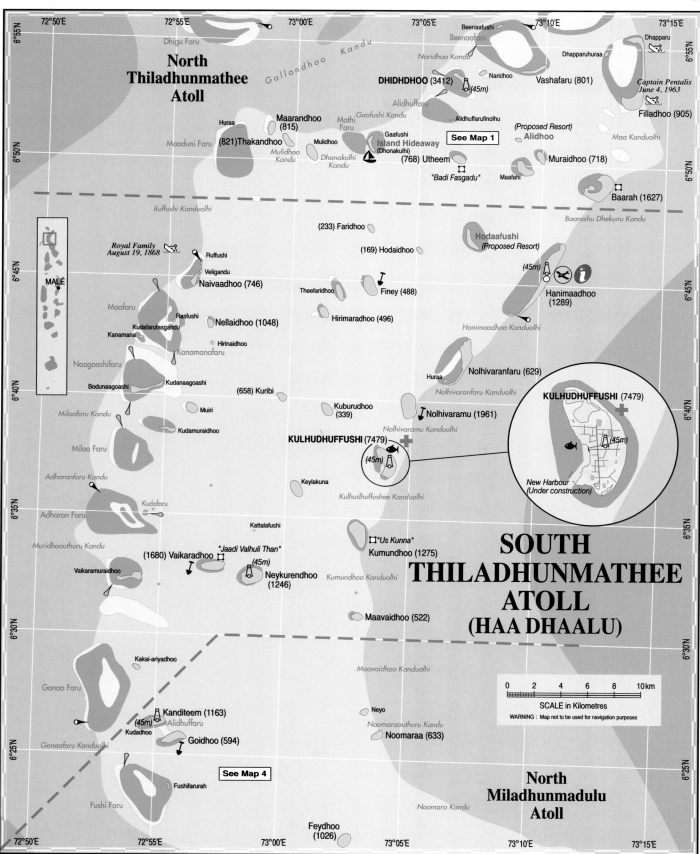

North
Thiladhunmathee
Atoll

Dhigu Faru

Gallandhoo Kandu

Beenaafushi
Beenaafaru

Dhapparu

Naridhoo Kandu

Dhapparuhuraa

DHIDHDHOO (3412)
(45m)

Naridhoo

Vashafaru (801)

*Captain Pentalis
June 4, 1963*

Huraa

Maarandhoo
(815)

Gaafushi Kandu

Alidhuffaru

Alidhuffarufinolhu

Filladhoo (905)

(821)Thakandhoo

Maaduni Faru

Mulidhoo

Gaafushi
Island Hideaway
(Dhonakulhi)

(Proposed Resort)
Alidhoo

Maa Kanduolhi

*Mulidhoo
Kandu*

*Dhonakulhi
Kandu*

(768) Utheem

See Map 1

Muraidhoo (718)

"Badi Fasgadu"

Maafahi

Baarah (1627)

Ruffushi Kanduolhi

Baarashu Dhekunu Kandu

(233) Faridhoo

Hodaafushi
(Proposed Resort)

*Royal Family
August 19, 1868*

Ruffushi

(169) Hodaidhoo

(45m)

MALÉ

Veligandu

Naivaadhoo (746)

Theefaridhoo

Finey (488)

Hanimaadhoo
(1289)

Maafaru

Rasfushi

Nellaidhoo (1048)

Hirimaradhoo (496)

Kudafarufasgandu

Kanamana

Hirinaidhoo

Hanimaadhoo Kanduolhi

Kanamanafaru

Naagooshifaru

Bodunaagoashi

Kudanaagoashi

(658) Kuribi

Huraa

Nolhivaranfaru (629)

Nolhivaranfaru Kanduolhi

KULHUDHUFFUSHI (7479)

Muiri

Kuburudhoo
(339)

Nolhivaramu (1961)

Milaafaru Kandu

Kudamuraidhoo

Nolhivaramu Kanduolhi

(45m)

Milaa Faru

KULHUDHUFFUSHI (7479)
(45m)

Adharanfaru Kandu

Keylakuna

*New Harbour
(Under construction)*

Kulhudhuffushee Kanduolhi

Adharan Faru

Kudafaru

Muridhoothuru Kandu

Kattalafushi

(1680) Vaikaradhoo

"Jaadi Valhuli Than"

(45m)

"Us Kunna"

Kumundhoo (1275)

SOUTH
THILADHUNMATHEE
ATOLL
(HAA DHAALU)

Vaikaramuraidhoo

Neykurendhoo
(1246)

Kumundhoo Kanduolhi

Maavaidhoo (522)

Maavaidhoo Kanduolhi

Kakai-ariyadhoo

Neyo

Gonaa Faru

Kanditeem (1163)
(45m)
Alidhuffaru
Kudadhoo

Goidhoo (594)

Noomaraa (633)

Noomaraauthuru Kandu

Gonaafaru Kanduolhi

See Map 4

North
Miladhunmadulu
Atoll

Fushifarurah

Noomara Kandu

Fushi Faru

Feydhoo
(1026)

| 0 | 2 | 4 | 6 | 8 | 10km |

SCALE in Kilometres
WARNING : Map not to be used for navigation purposes

MAP 4

SHAVIYANI

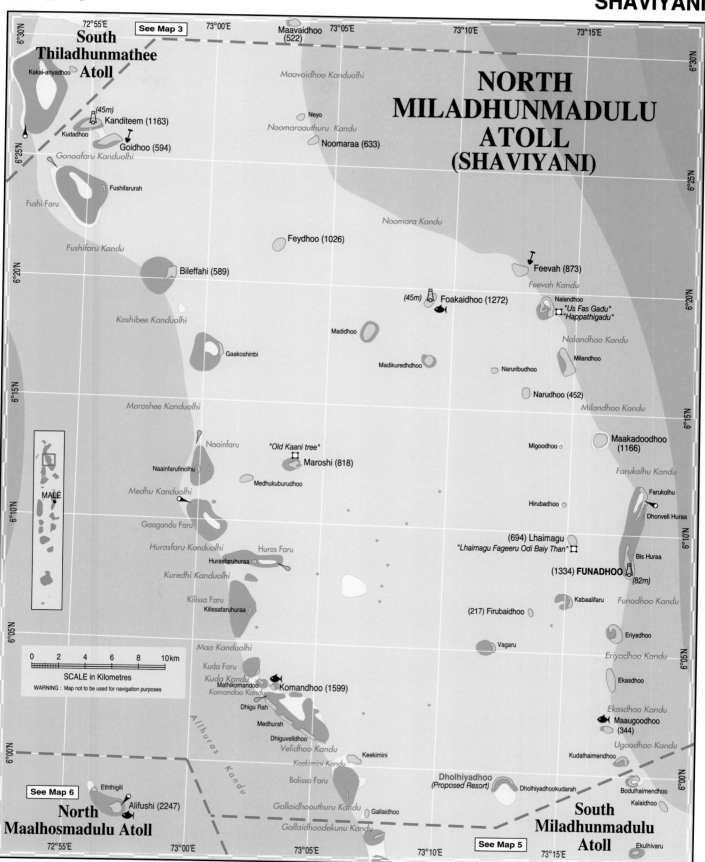

South
Thiladhunmathee
Atoll

See Map 3

Maavaidhoo
(522)

Maavaidhoo Kanduolhi

**NORTH
MILADHUNMADULU
ATOLL
(SHAVIYANI)**

Kakai-ariyadhoo

Neyo

Noomaraauthuru Kandu

(45m)

Kanditeem (1163)

Kudadhoo

Goidhoo (594)

Noomaraa (633)

Fushifarurah

Gonaafaru Kanduolhi

Fushi Faru

Feydhoo (1026)

Noomara Kandu

Feevah (873)

Feevah Kandu

Fushifaru Kandu

Bileffahi (589)

(45m) Foakaidhoo (1272)

Nalandhoo

"Us Fas Gadu"
"Happathigadu"

Koshibee Kanduolhi

Madidhoo

Milandhoo

Gaakoshinbi

Madikuredhdhoo

Naruribudhoo

Nalandhoo Kandu

Narudhoo (452)

Milandhoo Kandu

Maroshee Kanduolhi

Migoodhoo

Maakadoodhoo
(1166)

Naainfaru

"Old Kaani tree"

Farukolhu Kandu

Farukolhu

Naainfarufinolhu

Maroshi (818)

Medhukuburudhoo

Hirubadhoo

Dhonveli Huraa

Medhu Kanduolhi

MALÉ

(694) Lhaimagu
"Lhaimagu Fageeru Odi Baiy Than"

Bis Huraa

Gaagandu Faru

Hurasfaru Kanduolhi

Huras Faru

(1334) **FUNADHOO**

(82m)

Hurastaruhuraa

Kabaalifaru

Funadhoo Kandu

Kuredhi Kanduolhi

(217) Firubaidhoo

Eriyadhoo

Kilissa Faru

Kilissafaruhuraa

Eriyadhoo Kandu

Vagaru

Ekasdhoo

Maa Kanduolhi

Kuda Faru

Ekasdhoo Kandu

Maaugoodhoo
(344)

Kuda Kandu

Mathikomandoo

Komandhoo (1599)

Komandoo Kandu

Dhigu Rah

Ugoodhoo Kandu

Kudalhaimendhoo

Medhurah

Dhiguvelldhoo

Velidhoo Kandu

Keekimini

Dholhiyadhoo
(Proposed Resort)

Dholhiyadhookudarah

Bodulhaimendhoo

Keekimini Kandu

Kalaidhoo

See Map 6

Eththigili

Bolissa Faru

North
Maalhosmadulu Atoll

Alifushi (2247)

Gallaidhoouthuru Kandu

Gallaidhoo

South
Miladhunmadulu
Atoll

Gallaidhoodekunu Kandu

See Map 5

Ekulhivaru

0 2 4 6 8 10km

SCALE in Kilometres

WARNING : Map not to be used for navigation purposes

Allhuras Kandu

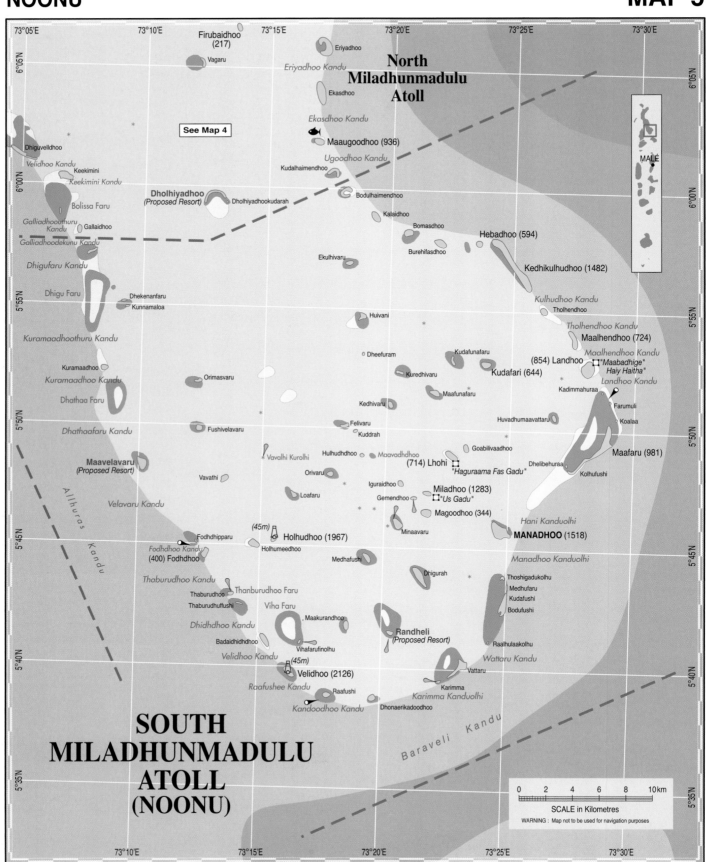

NOONU

MAP 5

Firubaidhoo (217)

Vagaru

Eriyadhoo

Eriyadhoo Kandu

North Miladhunmadulu Atoll

Ekasdhoo

Ekasdhoo Kandu

See Map 4

Maaugoodhoo (936)

Kudalhaimendhoo

Ugoodhoo Kandu

Dhiguvelldhoo

Velidhoo Kandu

Keekimini

Keekimini Kandu

Bolissa Faru

Galliadhoothuru Kandu

Gallaidhoo

Galliadhoodekunu Kandu

Dholhiyadhoo *(Proposed Resort)*

Dholhiyadhookudarah

Bodulhaimendhoo

Kalaidhoo

Bomasdhoo

Hebadhoo (594)

Dhigufaru Kandu

Ekulhivaru

Burehifasdhoo

Kedhikulhudhoo (1482)

Dhigu Faru

Dhekenanfaru

Kunnamaloa

Huivani

Kulhudhoo Kandu

Tholhendhoo

Tholhendhoo Kandu

Kuramaadhoothuru Kandu

Dheefuram

Kudafunafaru

Maalhendhoo (724)

Maalhendhoo Kandu

(854) Landhoo

"Maabadhige" Haiy Haitha"

Kuramaadhoo

Kuramaadhoo Kandu

Orimasvaru

Kuredhivaru

Kudafari (644)

Dhathaa Faru

Kedhivaru

Maafunafaru

Kadimmahuraa

Farumuli

Koalaa

Dhathaafaru Kandu

Fushivelavaru

Felivaru

Kuddrah

Huvadhumaavattaru

Landhoo Kandu

Maavelavaru *(Proposed Resort)*

Vavalhi Kurolhi

Hulhudhdhoo

Maavadhdhoo

Goabilivaadhoo

Maafaru (981)

(714) Lhohi

"Haguraama Fas Gadu"

Dhelibehuraa

Kolhufushi

Vavathi

Orivaru

Iguraidhoo

Miladhoo (1283)

"Us Gadu"

Velavaru Kandu

Loafaru

Gemendhoo

Magoodhoo (344)

Hani Kanduolhi

(45m)

Holhudhoo (1967)

Holhumeedhoo

Minaavaru

MANADHOO (1518)

Fodhdhipparu

Fodhdhoo Kandu

(400) **Fodhdhoo**

Medhafushi

Dhigurah

Manadhoo Kanduolhi

Thoshigadukolhu

Medhufaru

Kudafushi

Bodufushi

Thaburudhoo Kandu

Thanburudhoo Faru

Thaburudhoo

Thaburudhuffushi

Viha Faru

Maakurandhoo

Randheli

(Proposed Resort)

Raalhulaakolhu

Dhidhdhoo Kandu

Badaidhidhdhoo

Vihafarufinolhu

Velidhoo Kandu

(45m)

Velidhoo (2126)

Vattaru

Wattaru Kandu

Raafushee Kandu

Raafushi

Karimma

Karimma Kanduolhi

Kandoodhoo Kandu

Dhonaerikadoodhoo

Baraveli Kandu

SOUTH MILADHUNMADULU ATOLL (NOONU)

Allhuras Kandu

MALÉ

SCALE in Kilometres

0 2 4 6 8 10km

WARNING : Map not to be used for navigation purposes

MAP 6

RAA

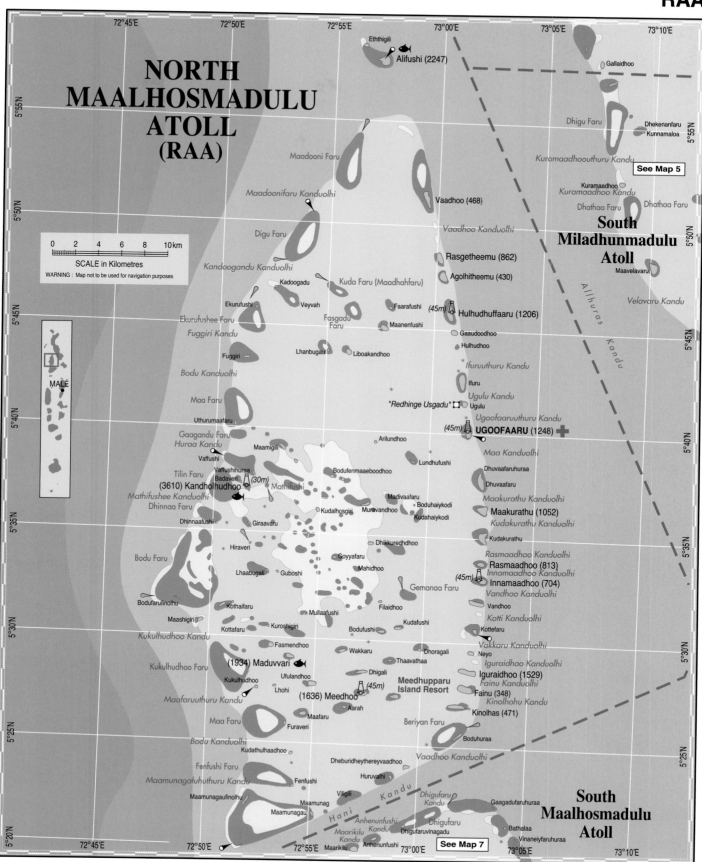

NORTH
MAALHOSMADULU
ATOLL
(RAA)

Eththigili
Alifushi (2247)
Gallaidhoo

Maadooni Faru
Dhigu Faru
Dhekenanfaru
Kunnamaloa

Maadoonifaru Kanduolhi
Vaadhoo (468)
Kuramaadhoouthuru Kandu
See Map 5

Digu Faru
Vaadhoo Kanduolhi
Kuramaadhoo
Kuramaadhoo Kandu

**South
Miladhunmadulu
Atoll**

Kandoogandu Kanduolhi
Rasgetheemu (862)
Dhathaa Faru
Dhathaa Faru

Kadoogadu
Agolhitheemu (430)
Maavelavaru

Ekurufushi
Veyvah
Kuda Faru (Maadhahfaru)
Faarafushi
(45m)
Hulhudhuffaaru (1206)
Velavaru Kandu

Ekurufushee Faru
Fasgadu Faru
Maanenfushi
Gaaudoodhoo

Fuggiri Kandu
Hulhudhoo

Bodu Kanduolhi
Lhanbugadu
Liboakandhoo
Ifuruuthuru Kandu

Fuggiri
Ifuru
Ugulu Kandu

Maa Faru
"Redhinge Usgadu"
Ugulu

Uthurumaafaru
Arilundhoo
Ugoofaaruuthuru Kandu

Gaagandu Faru
(45m) **UGOOFAARU** (1248)
Huraa Kandu

Vaffushi
Maamigili
Lundhufushi
Maa Kanduolhi

Tilin Faru
Vaffushihuraa
Badaveri
Bodufenmaaeeboodhoo
Dhuvaafaruhuraa

(3610) Kandholhudhoo
(30m)
Dhuvaafaru

Mathifushee Kanduolhi
Mathifushi
Madivaafaru
Maakurathu Kanduolhi

Dhinnaa Faru
Kudalhosgiri
Muravandhoo
Boduhaiykodi
Maakurathu (1052)

Dhinnaafushi
Giraavuru
Kudahaiykodi
Kudakurathu Kanduolhi

Hiraveri
Dhikkuredhdhoo
Kudakurathu

Bodu Faru
Goyyafaru
Rasmaadhoo Kanduolhi

Lhaabugali
Guboshi
Mahidhoo
Rasmaadhoo (813)

Bodufarufinolhu
Gemanaa Faru
(45m)
Innamaadhoo (704)
Innamaadhoo Kanduolhi

Kothaifaru
Filaidhoo
Vandhoo
Vandhoo Kanduolhi

Maashigiri
Mullaafushi
Kudafushi
Kotti Kanduolhi

Kottafaru
Kuroshigiri
Bodufushi
Kottefaru

Kukulhudhoo Kandu
Fasmendhoo
Dhoragali
Neyo
Vakkaru Kanduolhi

Kukulhudhoo Faru
Wakkaru
Thaavathaa
Iguraidhoo (1529)
Iguraidhoo Kanduolhi

(1934) Maduvvari
Dhigali
Iguraidhoo
Fainu Kanduolhi

Kukulhudhoo
Ufulandhoo
Meedhupparu
Island Resort
Fainu (348)

Lhohi
(45m)
Kinolhohu Kandu

Maafaruuthuru Kandu
(1636) Meedhoo
Kinolhas (471)

Maafaru
Aarah
Kinolhohu Kandu

Furaveri

Maa Faru
Beriyan Faru

Bodu Kanduolhi
Boduhuraa

Kudathulhaadhoo
Dheburidheythereyvaadhoo
Vaadhoo Kanduolhi

Fenfushi Faru
Huruvalhi

Maamunagaluhuthuru Kandu
Fenfushi
Viligili
Hani Kandu
Dhigufaru Kandu
Gaagadufaruhuraa

Maamunagaufinolhu
Maamunag
Maarikilu Kandu
Dhigufaru
**South
Maalhosmadulu
Atoll**

Maamunagau
Anhenunfushi Kandu
Dhigufaruvinagadu
Bathalaa

Maarikilu
Anhenunfushi
See Map 7
Vinaneiyfaruhuraa

MALÉ

0 2 4 6 8 10km
SCALE in Kilometres
WARNING : Map not to be used for navigation purposes

23

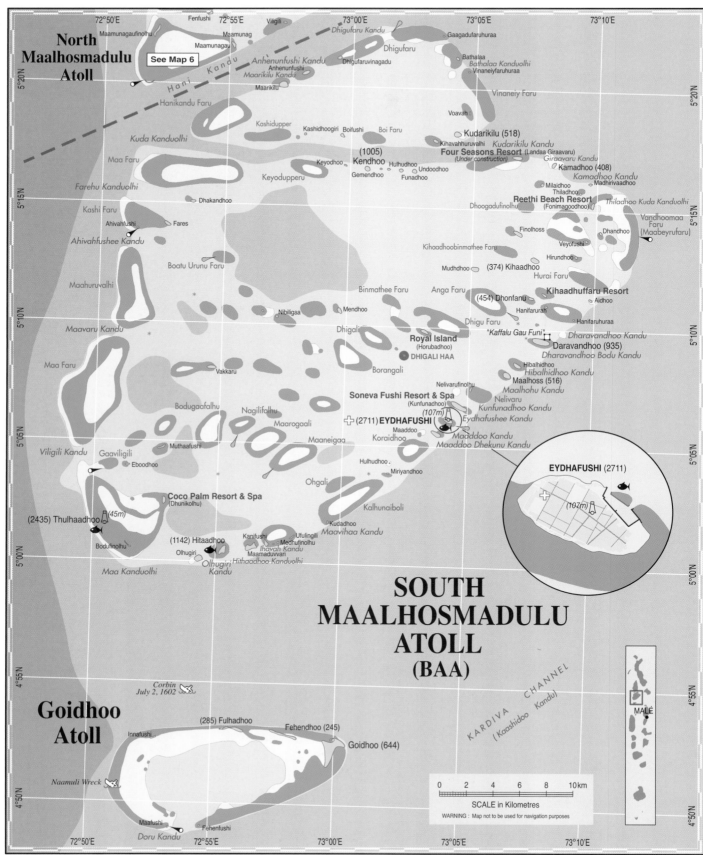

North
Maalhosmadulu
Atoll

See Map 6

Fenfushi
Viligili
Maamunagaufinolhu
Maamunag
Maamunagau

Dhigufaru Kandu
Gaagadufaruhuraa
Dhigufaru
Anhenunfushi Kandu
Anhenunfushi
Dhigufaruvinagadu
Bathalaa
Bathalaa Kanduolhi
Maarikilu Kandu
Vinaneiyfaruhuraa
Maarikilu
Hani *Kandu*
Hanikandu Faru
Vinaneiy Faru
Voavah
Kuda Kanduolhi
Kashidupper
Kashidhoogiri
Boifushi
Boi Faru
Kudarikilu (518)
Kihavahhuruvalhi
Kudarikilu Kandu
Four Seasons Resort (Landaa Giraavaru)
(Under construction)
Giraavaru Kandu
Kamadhoo (408)
Kamadhoo Kandu
Madhirivaadhoo
Maa Faru
(1005)
Kendhoo
Keyodhoo
Hulhudhoo
Undoodhoo
Milaidhoo
Thiladhoo
Keyodupperu
Gemendhoo
Funadhoo
Reethi Beach Resort
(Fonimagoodhoo)
Thiladhoo Kuda Kanduolhi
Farehu Kanduolhi
Dhoogadufinolhu
Finolhoss
Dhandhoo
Vandhoomaa Faru (Maabeyrufaru)
Kashi Faru
Dhakandhoo
Veyofushi
Ahivahfushi
Fares
Hirundhoo
Ahivahfushee Kandu
Kihaadhoobinmathee Faru
Boatu Urunu Faru
Mudhdhoo
(374) Kihaadhoo
Hurai Faru
Maahuruvalhi
Binmathee Faru
Anga Faru
(454) Dhonfanu
Kihaadhuffaru Resort
Hanifarurah
Aidhoo
Maavaru Kandu
Nibiligaa
Mendhoo
Dhigali
Dhigu Faru
Hanifaruhuraa
"Kaffalu Gau Funi"
Dharavandhoo Kandu
Maa Faru
Vakkaru
Royal Island
(Horubadhoo)
Borangali
Daravandhoo (935)
Dharavandhoo Bodu Kandu
Hibalhidhoo
Hibalhidhoo Kandu
● **DHIGALI HAA**
Maalhoss (516)
Bodugaafalhu
Nagilifalhu
Nelivarufinolhu
Nelivaru
Maalhohu Kandu
Soneva Fushi Resort & Spa
(Kunfunadhoo)
Kunfunadhoo Kandu
Maarogaali
(107m)
✚ (2711) **EYDHAFUSHI**
Eydhafushee Kandu
Viligili Kandu
Gaaviligili
Muthaafushi
Maaneigaa
Maaddoo
Koraidhoo
Maaddoo Kandu
Maaddoo Dhekunu Kandu
Eboodhoo
Hulhudhoo
EYDHAFUSHI (2711)
Miriyandhoo
✚
(107m)
Ohgali
(2435) Thulhaadhoo
(45m)
Coco Palm Resort & Spa
(Dhunikolhu)
Kalhunaiboli
Bodufinolhu
(1142) Hitaadhoo
Kanifushi
Ufulingili
Medhufinolhi
Kudadhoo
Maavihaa Kandu
Olhugiri
Ihavah Faru
Maamaduvvari
Olhugiri Kandu
Hithaadhoo Kanduolhi
Maa Kanduolhi

SOUTH
MAALHOSMADULU
ATOLL
(BAA)

**Goidhoo
Atoll**

Corbin
July 2, 1602
Innafushi
(285) Fulhadhoo
Fehendhoo (245)
Goidhoo (644)

KARDIVA *CHANNEL*
(Kaashidoo Kandu)

MALÉ

Naamuli Wreck

Maafushi
Fehenfushi
Doru Kandu

0   2   4   6   8   10km
SCALE in Kilometres
WARNING : Map not to be used for navigation purposes

MAP 8

LHAVIYANI

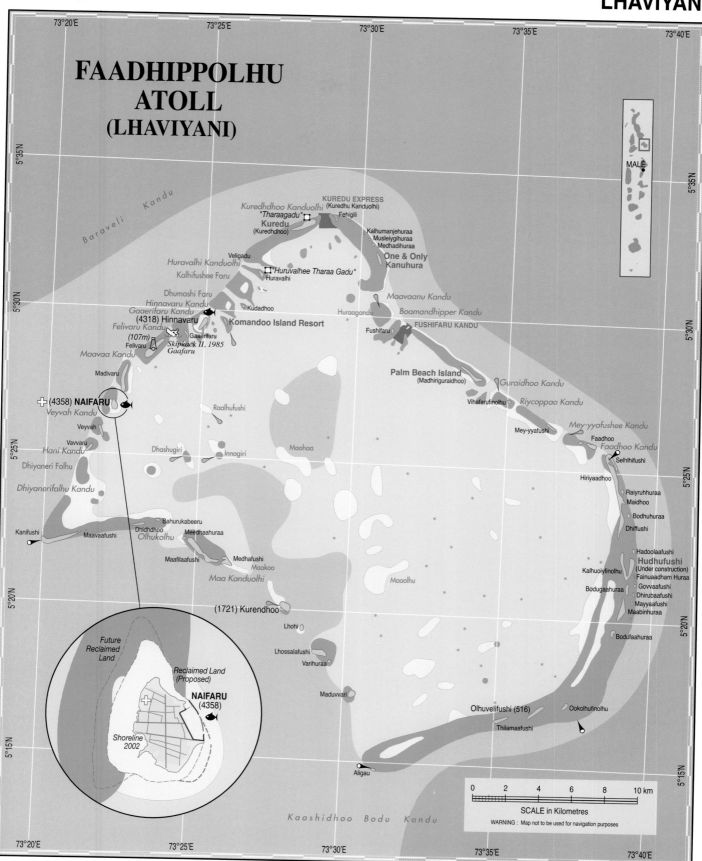

FAADHIPPOLHU ATOLL
(LHAVIYANI)

MALÉ

Baraveli Kandu

Kuredhdhoo Kanduolhi
KUREDU EXPRESS
(Kuredhu Kanduolhi)
"Tharaagadu"
Kuredu
(Kuredhdhoo)
Fehigili

Kalhumanjehuraa
Musleiygihuraa
Medhadihuraa

One & Only
Kanuhura

Veligadu

Huravalhi Kanduolhi
Kalhifushee Faru
"Huruvalhee Tharaa Gadu"
Huravalhi

Dhumashi Faru
Hinnavaru Kandu
Gaaerifaru Kandu
(4318) Hinnavaru
Felivaru Kandu
(107m)
Felivaru
Kudadhoo

Gaaerifaru
Skipkack II, 1985
Gaafaru

Maavaa Kandu

Komandoo Island Resort

Huraagandu

Maavaanu Kandu
Boamandhipper Kandu

Fushifaru
FUSHIFARU KANDU

Madivaru

Palm Beach Island
(Madhiriguraidhoo)

Guraidhoo Kandu

Vihafarufinolhu
Riycoppaa Kandu

Mey-yyafushee Kandu

✛ (4358) NAIFARU
Veyvah Kandu

Veyvah

Raalhufushi

Mey-yyafushi

Faadhoo
Faadhoo Kandu

Selhlhifushi

Vavvaru
Hani Kandu

Dhashugiri
Innagiri

Maahaa

Hiriyaadhoo

Raiyruhhuraa
Maidhoo

Dhiyaneri Falhu

Dhiyanerifalhu Kandu

Maahaa

Bodhuhuraa

Dhiffushi

Kanifushi
Maavaafushi
Dhidhdhoo
Olhukolhu
Bahurukabeeru
Meedhaahuraa

Maafilaafushi
Medhafushi
Maakoa

Maa Kanduolhi

Maaolhu

Hadoolaafushi
Hudhufushi
(Under construction)
Kalhuoiyfinolhu
Fainuaadham Huraa
Govvaafushi
Bodugaahuraa
Dhirubaafushi
Mayyaafushi
Maabinhuraa

Bodufaahuraa

(1721) Kurendhoo

Lhohi

Lhossalafushi
Varihuraa

Maduvvari

Olhuvelifushi (516)
Thilamaafushi

Ookolhufinolhu

Aligau

(inset)
Future
Reclaimed
Land

Reclaimed Land
(Proposed)

✛ NAIFARU
(4358)

Shoreline
2002

| 0 | 2 | 4 | 6 | 8 | 10 km |

SCALE in Kilometres
WARNING : Map not to be used for navigation purposes

Kaashidhoo Bodu Kandu

73°20'E 73°25'E 73°30'E 73°35'E 73°40'E
5°35'N 5°30'N 5°25'N 5°20'N 5°15'N

1 The airport island of Hulhule, Kaafu.
2 Faadhoo, an uninhabited island in Lhaviyani. 3 The Wreck of the Skipjack II, Lhavyani.
4 The Wreck of the Erlangen, Gaafaru. 5 The Wreck of the Lady Christine, Gaafaru. 6 The anchor of the SS Sea Gull, Gaafaru.

MAP 9

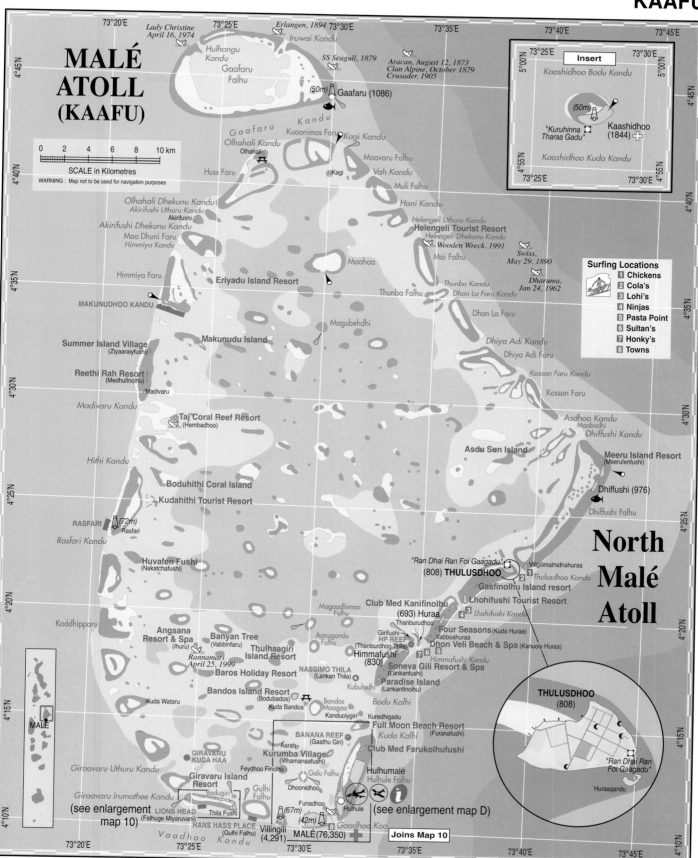

MALÉ ATOLL (KAAFU)

Lady Christine April 16, 1974

Erlangen, 1894

Iruwai Kandu

SS Seagull, 1879

Aracan, August 12, 1873
Clan Alpine, October 1879
Crusader, 1905

Hulhangu Kandu

Gaafaru Falhu

(50m) Gaafaru (1086)

Gaafaru Kandu

Kuoonimas Faru

Kagi Kandu

Insert

Kaashidhoo Bodu Kandu

(50m)

"Kuruhinna Tharaa Gadu"

Kaashidhoo (1844)

Kaashidhoo Kuda Kandu

Olhahali Kandu
Olhahali

Kagi

Maavaru Falhu

Vah Kandu

Muli Falhu

SCALE in Kilometres

0 2 4 6 8 10 km

WARNING : Map not to be used for navigation purposes

Huss Faru

Hani Kandu

Olhahali Dhekunu Kandu
Akirifushi Uthuru Kandu
Akirifushi

Helengeli Uthuru Kandu
Helengeli Tourist Resort
Helengeli Dhekunu Kandu
Wooden Wreck, 1991

Akirifushi Dhekunu Kandu
Maa Dhuni Faru
Himmiya Kandu

Mai Falhu

Swiss, May 29, 1890

Himmiya Faru

Eriyadu Island Resort

Maahaa

Thunba Kandu
Dhon La Faru Kandu

Dharuma, Jan 24, 1962

MAKUNUDHOO KANDU

Thunba Falhu

Surfing Locations

1	Chickens
2	Cola's
3	Lohi's
4	Ninjas
5	Pasta Point
6	Sultan's
7	Honky's
8	Towns

Magubehdhi

Dhon La Faru

Dhiya Adi Kandu

Dhiya Adi Faru

Summer Island Village
(Ziyaaraiyfushi)

Makunudu Island

Reethi Rah Resort
(Medhufinolhu)

Madivaru

Kassan Faru Kandu

Kassan Faru

Madivaru Kandu

Taj Coral Reef Resort
(Hembadhoo)

Asdhoo Kandu
Maabadhi
Dhiffushi Kandu

Hithi Kandu

Asdu Sun Island

Meeru Island Resort
(Meerufenfushi)

Boduhithi Coral Island

Kudahithi Tourist Resort

Dhiffushi (976)

RASFARI (72m)
Rasfari

Dhiffushi Falhu

Rasfari Kandu

Huvafen Fushi
(Nakatchafushi)

"Ran Dhai Ran Foi Gaagadu"
(808) **THULUSDHOO**

Viligilimathidhahuraa

North Malé Atoll

Thulusdhoo Kandu

Gasfinolhu Island resort

Lhohifushi Tourist Resort

Koddhipparu

Club Med Kanifinolhu
(693) **Huraa**

Lhohifushi Kandu

Magaadhimaa Falhu

Thanburdhoo

Four Seasons (Kuda Huraa)
Vabboahuraa

Angsana Resort & Spa
(Ihuru)

Banyan Tree
(Vabbinfaru)

Aanugandu Falhu

Girifushi
HP REEF
(Thanburdhoo Thila)

Himmafushi

Dhon Veli Beach & Spa (Kanuoiy Huraa)

Rannamari April 25, 1999

Thulhaagiri Island Resort

Himmafushi
(830)

Soneva Gili Resort & Spa
(Lankanfushi)

THULUSDHOO
(808)

Baros Holiday Resort

NASSIMO THILA
(Lankan Thila)

Paradise Island
(Lankanfinolhu)

Kubuladhi

Bandos Island Resort
(Bodubados)

Kuda Bandos

Bandos Maagaa

Kanduoiygiri

Bodu Kalhi

Kuda Wataru

Kuredhigadu

Full Moon Beach Resort
(Furanafushi)

Ran Dhai Ran Foi Gaagadu

MALÉ

BANANA REEF
(Gaathu Giri)

Kuda Kalhi

Club Med Farukolhufushi

Huraagandu

GIRAAVARU KUDA HAA

Aarah

Kurumba Village
(Vihamanaafushi)

Feydhoo Finolhu

Galu Falhu

Dhoonidhoo

Hulhumalé
Hulhule Falhu

Giraavaru Uthuru Kandu

Giraavaru Island Resort
Bodugiri

Gulhi Falhu

(see enlargement map D)

Giraavaru Irumathee Kandu

Thila Fushi

LIONS HEAD
(Falhuge Miyaruvani)

Funadhoo

(67m)

Hulhule

(see enlargement map 10)

HANS HASS PLACE
(Gulhi Falhu)

Villingili
(4,291)

(42m)

MALÉ (76,350)

Gaadhoo Koa

Vaadhoo Kandu

Joins Map 10

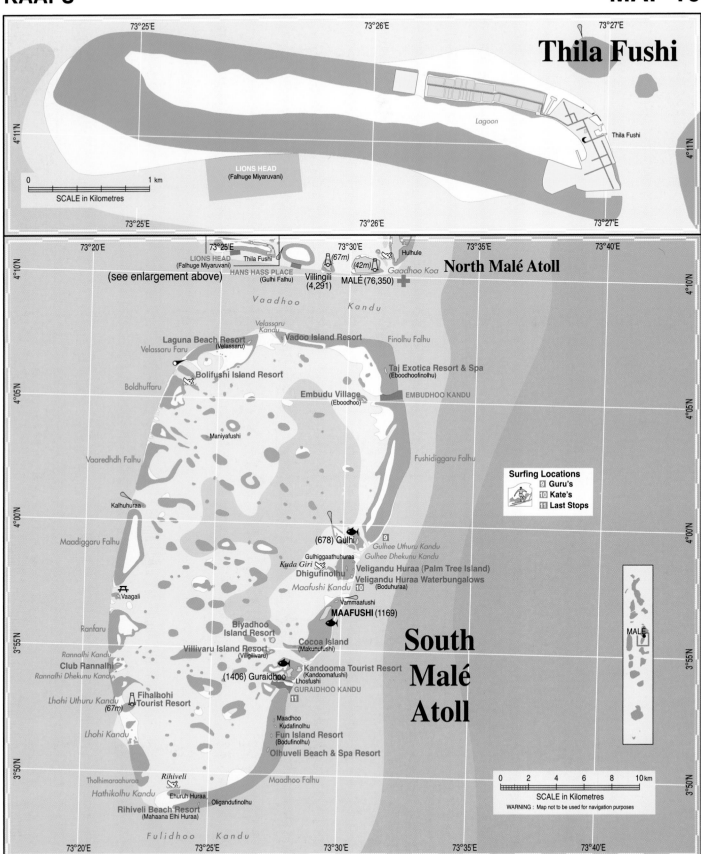

Thila Fushi

73°25'E 73°26'E 73°27'E

4°11'N

Lagoon

Thila Fushi

LIONS HEAD
(Falhuge Miyaruvani)

0   1 km
SCALE in Kilometres

73°25'E 73°26'E 73°27'E

73°20'E 73°25'E 73°30'E 73°35'E 73°40'E

4°10'N

LIONS HEAD
(Falhuge Miyaruvani) Thila Fushi

Hulhule

(67m)

(42m)

North Malé Atoll

(see enlargement above) HANS HASS PLACE
(Gulhi Falhu) Villingili
(4,291) MALÉ (76,350) Gaadhoo Koa

Vaadhoo Kandu

Velassaru
Kandu

Laguna Beach Resort
(Velassaru) **Vadoo Island Resort** Finolhu Falhu

Velassaru Faru

Taj Exotica Resort & Spa
(Eboodhoofinolhu)

Boldhuffaru **Bolifushi Island Resort**

4°05'N

Embudu Village
(Eboodhoo) EMBUDHOO KANDU

Maniyafushi

Fushidiggaru Falhu

Vaaredhdh Falhu

Surfing Locations
9 Guru's
10 Kate's
11 Last Stops

4°00'N

Kalhuhuraa

Maadiggaru Falhu

(678) Gulhi

Gulhee Uthuru Kandu
Gulhee Dhekunu Kandu **9**

Gulhiggaathuhuraa

Kuda Giri
Dhigufinolhu

Veligandu Huraa (Palm Tree Island)
Veligandu Huraa Waterbungalows
(Boduhuraa)

Maafushi Kandu **10**

MALÉ

Vaagali

Vammaafushi

MAAFUSHI (1169)

Ranfaru

**Biyadhoo
Island Resort**

3°55'N

Cocoa Island
(Makunufushi)

Villivaru Island Resort
(Villgilivaru)

Rannalhi Kandu **Kandooma Tourist Resort**
(Kandoomafushi)

Club Rannalhi (1406) Guraidhoo Lhosfushi

Rannalhi Dhekunu Kandu GURAIDHOO KANDU

Lhohi Uthuru Kandu **Fihalhohi
Tourist Resort** **11**

(67m)

Lhohi Kandu Maadhoo
Kudafinolhu

Fun Island Resort
(Bodufinolhu)

3°50'N

Rihiveli **Olhuveli Beach & Spa Resort**

Tholhimaraahuraa

Hathikolhu Kandu Ehuruh Huraa Oligandufinolhu *Maadhoo Falhu*

**South
Malé
Atoll**

Rihiveli Beach Resort
(Mahaana Elhi Huraa)

Fulidhoo Kandu

0 2 4 6 8 10km
SCALE in Kilometres
WARNING : Map not to be used for navigation purposes

73°20'E 73°25'E 73°30'E 73°35'E 73°40'E

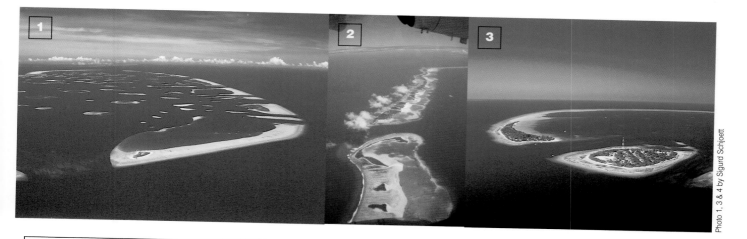

1 Islands of Kaafu, South Malé Atoll with Velassaru in the foreground.
2 Looking north at islands in Gaafu Dhaalu showing Fiyoaree Kandu.
3 Rasdhoo island (front) and Kuramathi, Alifu Alifu. **4** Islands of Alifu Dhaalu with Maamigili in foreground.

Photo courtesy Sigurd Schjoett

1
Looking south towards Helengeli in North Malé Atoll.

2
The regional airport of Hanimaadhoo in Haa Dhaalu

3
Dhonakulhi, is the first resort in Haa Alifu.
A proposed marina will cater for foreign yachts.

4
A near perfect circle.
The island of Alidhoo in Haa Alifu will become a resort.

Photo courtesy Island Aviation

Protected Marine Areas

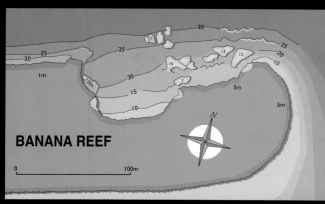

BANANA REEF 04°14.5' N 73°32' E MAP 9

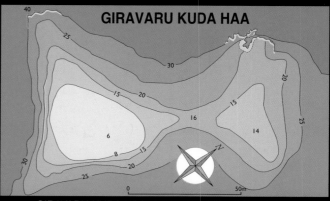

GIRAVARU KUDA HAA 04°12' N 73°24.5' E MAP 9

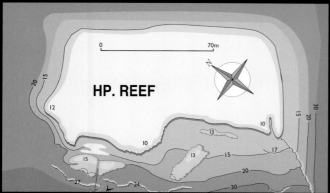

HP REEF 04°19' N 73°34.5' E MAP 9

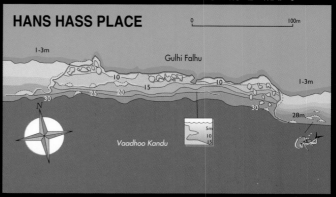

HANS HASS PLACE 04°10.5' N 73°28' E MAP 9

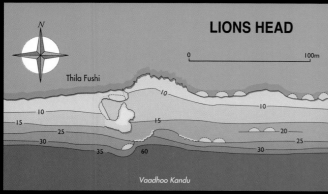

LIONS HEAD 04°11' N 73°25.5' E MAP 9

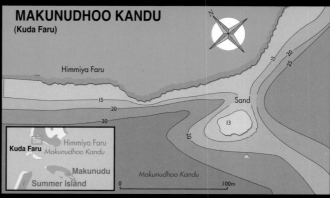

MAKUNUDHOO KANDU 04°34' N 73°23' E MAP 9

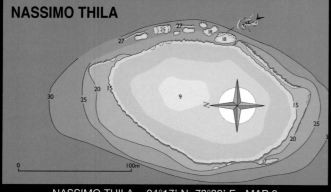

NASSIMO THILA 04°17' N 73°32' E MAP 9

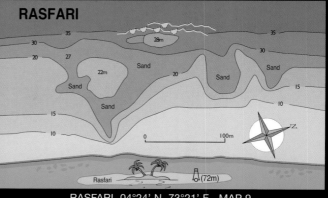

RASFARI 04°24' N 73°21' E MAP 9

Protected Marine Areas

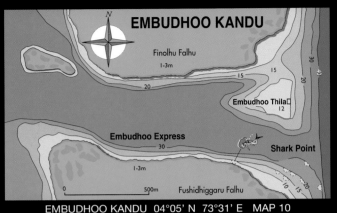

EMBUDHOO KANDU

N

Finolhu Falhu
1-3m

30
15   15
20
40
20

Embudhoo Thila
12

Embudhoo Express
30

Shark Point

1-3m
Fushidhiggaru Falhu

10
20
15

0   500m

EMBUDHOO KANDU   04°05' N   73°31' E   MAP 10

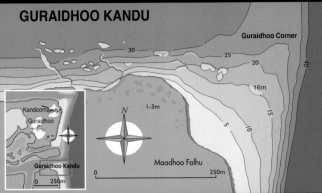

GURAIDHOO KANDU

Guraidhoo Corner
30   25
20
40
16m
15

Kandooma
Guraidhoo
1-3m
N
5
10

Guraidhoo Kandu
0   250m

Maadhoo Falhu

0   250m

GURAIDHOO KANDU   03°53.5' N   73°27' E   MAP 10

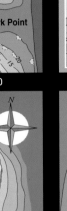

N

25
17   15   10

Hole   10

B   10   10

14

FISH HEAD

15
20
25

A
20
15
20
30

15
20
25
30

10
15
20

C

0   80m

FISH HEAD   03°56' N   72°55' E   MAP 11

KARI BEYRU THILA

N

30
25
15
12m

10m

8m   10m   10m

20
15   25
30

0   100m

KARIBEYRU THILA   04°06' N   72°57' E   MAP 11

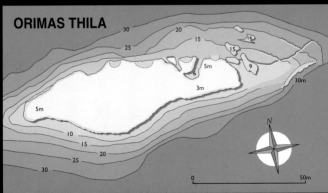

ORIMAS THILA

30   20
25   15   16
15
6   5m   9
3m

5m

10
15
20
25
30

30m

N

0   50m

ORIMAS THILA   03°59' N   72°57' E   MAP 11

11m
16   20

25   15
24   10   20
10
30
12
40
20   15   12
25   10
30   20
25
19m

MAAYA THILA

17

0   80m

MAAYA THILA   04°05' N   72°51.5' E   MAP 11

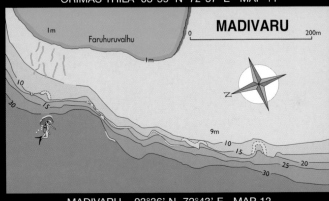

1m
Faruhuruvalhu
0

MADIVARU
200m

1m

10
30
15

9m
10
15
25   20
30

N

MADIVARU   03°36' N   72°43' E   MAP 12

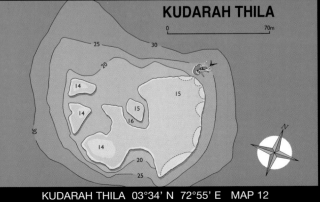

KUDARAH THILA
0   70m

25   30
20
14
15
14   15
16
30
14
20
25

N

KUDARAH THILA   03°34' N   72°55' E   MAP 12

Protected Marine Areas

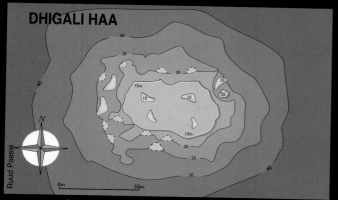

DHIGALI HAA

DHIGALI HAA 05°08'N 73°02' N   MAP 7

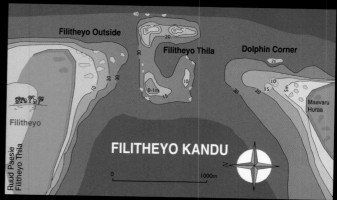

Filitheyo Outside

Filitheyo Thila

Dolphin Corner

Maavaru Huraa

Filitheyo

Ruud Paesie
Filitheyo Thila

FILITHEYO KANDU

FILITHEYO KANDU 03°13' N 73°02' E   MAP 14

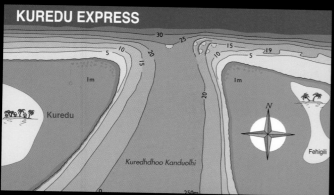

KUREDU EXPRESS

Kuredu

Kuredhdhoo Kanduolhi

Fehigili

KUREDU EXPRESS 05°33' N 73°28' E   MAP 8

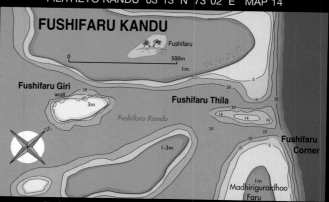

FUSHIFARU KANDU

Fushifaru

Fushifaru Giri
wall

Fushifaru Kandu

Fushifaru Thila

Fushifaru Corner

Madhiriguraidhoo Faru

FUSHIFARU KANDU 05°29' N 73°31' E   MAP 8

HAKURA THILA

0-2m

10m

Ruud Paesie

HAKURA THILA 02°57' N 73°33' E   MAP 16

FUSHI KANDU

Maavaru Falhu

Maadhiggaru Falhu

FUSHI KANDU 03°00' N 72°56' E   MAP 15

MIYARU KANDU (Devana Kandu)

Vihamaa Faru

Bodu Miyaru Kandu

Miyaru Kandu

Kudadhiggaru Falhu

MIYARU KANDU 03°34.5' N 73°30' E   MAP 13

Vattaru Falhu

Vattaru

Sand

VATTARU KANDU

Ruud Paesie

VATTARU KANDU 03°13' N 73°26' E   MAP 13

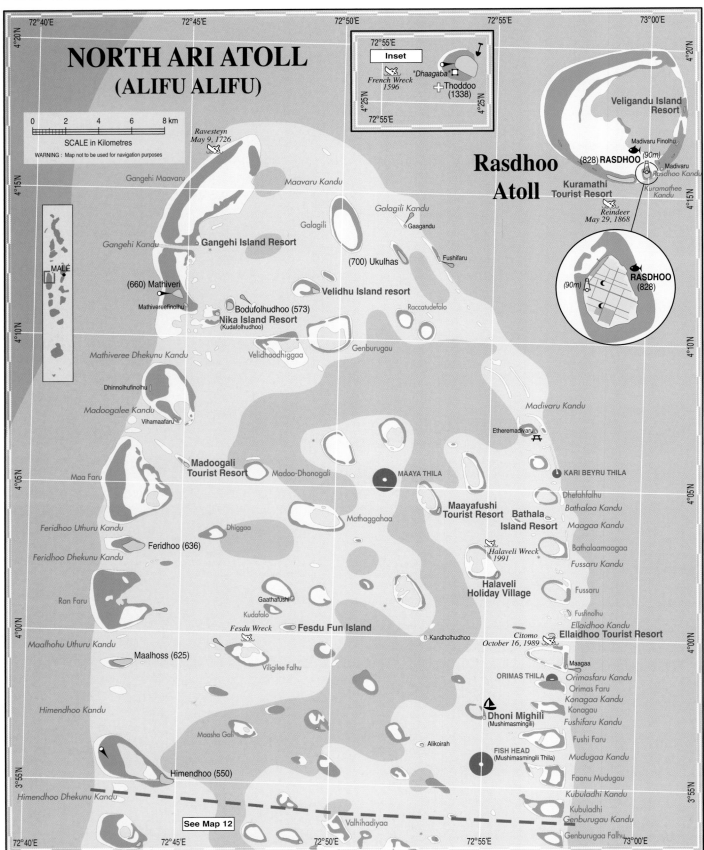

NORTH ARI ATOLL
(ALIFU ALIFU)

0   2   4   6   8 km

SCALE in Kilometres

WARNING : Map not to be used for navigation purposes

Inset

72°55'E

French Wreck 1596

"Dhaagaba"

✈ Thoddoo (1338)

Rasdhoo Atoll

Veligandu Island Resort

Madivaru Finolhu

(828) **RASDHOO**   (90m)   Madivaru

Rasdhoo Kandu

Kuramathi Tourist Resort

Kuramathee Kandu

Reindeer May 29, 1868

RASDHOO (828)

(90m)

Ravesteyn May 9, 1726

Gangehi Maavaru

Maavaru Kandu

Galagili Kandu

Galagili   • Gaagandu

Gangehi Island Resort

Gangehi Kandu

(700) Ukulhas   • Fushifaru

(660) Mathiveri

Mathivereefinolhu

Velidhu Island resort

Bodufolhudhoo (573)
Nika Island Resort
(Kudafolhudhoo)

Raccatudefalo

Velidhoodhiggaa   Genburugau

Mathiveree Dhekunu Kandu

Dhinnolhufinolhu

Madoogalee Kandu

Vihamaafaru

Madivaru Kandu

Etheremadivaru 🏕

Madoogali Tourist Resort   Madoo-Dhonogali   **MAAYA THILA**   **KARI BEYRU THILA**

Moa Faru

Dhefahfalhu

Maayafushi Tourist Resort   **Bathala Island Resort**

Bathalaa Kandu

Feridhoo Uthuru Kandu   Dhiggaa   Mathaggahaa   *Maagaa Kandu*

Feridhoo Dhekunu Kandu

Halaveli Wreck 1991

Bathalaamaagaa

Feridhoo (636)

Fussaru Kandu

Ran Faru

Halaveli Holiday Village   Fussaru

Gaathafushi

Kudafalo

• Fusfinolhu

Ellaidhoo Kandu

Fesdu Wreck ✈   **Fesdu Fun Island**

• Kandholhudhoo

Citomo October 16, 1989 ✈   **Ellaidhoo Tourist Resort**

Maalhohu Uthuru Kandu

Maalhoss (625)

Maagaa

Viligilee Falhu

ORIMAS THILA   *Orimasfaru Kandu*

Orimas Faru

Konagaa Kandu

Konagau

Dhoni Mighili
(Mushimasmingili)

Fushifaru Kandu

Himendhoo Kandu

Fushi Faru

Maasha Gali   • Alikoirah

FISH HEAD
(Mushimasmingili Thila)

Mudugaa Kandu

Himendhoo (550)   *Faanu Mudugau*

Kubuladhi Kandu

Himendhoo Dhekunu Kandu

Kubuladhi

Genburugau Kandu

See Map 12   Valhihadiyaa   *Genburugaa Falhu*

MALÉ

MAP 12

ALIFU DHAALU

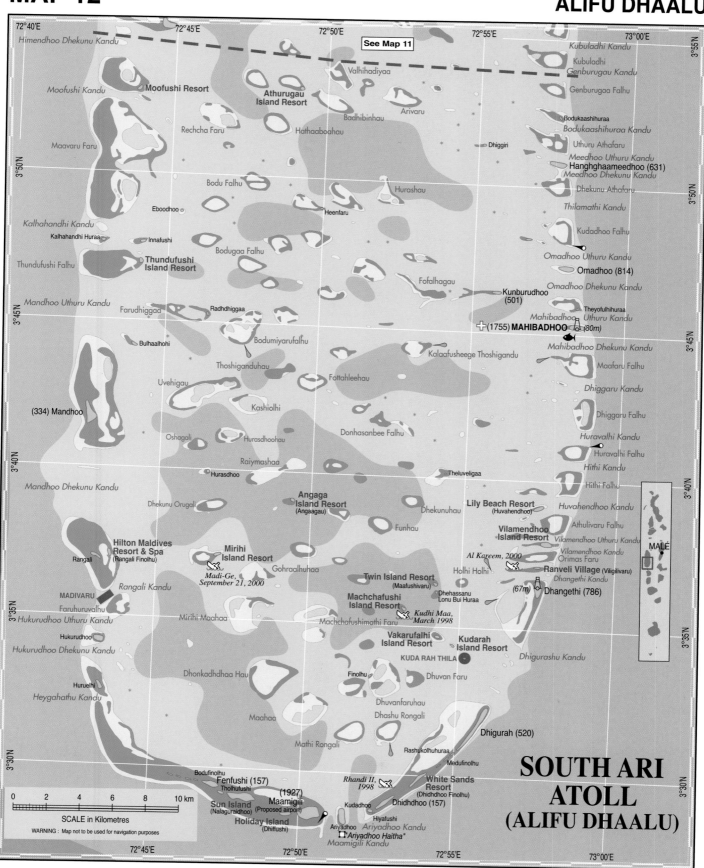

See Map 11

Himendhoo Dhekunu Kandu

Moofushi Kandu
Moofushi Resort
Valhihadiyaa
Kubuladhi Kandu
Kubuladhi
Genburugau Kandu
Genburugaa Falhu

Athurugau
Island Resort
Badhibinhau
Arivaru

Maavaru Faru
Rechcha Faru
Hathaaboahau
Dhiggiri
Bodukaashihuraa
Bodukaashihuraa Kandu
Uthuru Athafaru
Meedhoo Uthuru Kandu
Hanghghaameedhoo (631)
Meedhoo Dhekunu Kandu

Bodu Falhu
Hurashau
Dhekunu Athafaru

Eboodhoo
Heenfaru
Thilamathi Kandu

Kalhahandhi Kandu
Innafushi
Kudadhoo Falhu

Kalhahandhi Huraa
Bodugaa Falhu
Fofalhagau
Omadhoo Uthuru Kandu

Thundufushi Falhu
Thundufushi
Island Resort
Omadhoo (814)

Kunburudhoo
(501)
Omadhoo Dhekunu Kandu

Mandhoo Uthuru Kandu
Farudhiggaa
Radhdhiggaa
Theyofulhihuraa

Mahibadhoo Uthuru Kandu
✚ (1755) **MAHIBADHOO** 🐟 (80m)

Bulhaalhohi
Bodumiyarufalhu
Kalaafusheege Thoshigandu
Mahibadhoo Dhekunu Kandu

Thoshiganduhau
Fottahleehau
Maafaru Falhu

Uvehigau
Dhiggaru Kandu

Kashiolhi
Dhiggaru Falhu

(334) Mandhoo
Oshagali
Hurasdhoohau
Donhasanbee Falhu
Huravalhi Kandu

Raiymashaa
Huravalhi Falhu

Mandhoo Dhekunu Kandu
Hurasdhoo
Theluveligaa
Hithi Kandu

Hithi Falhu

Dhekunu Orugali
Angaga
Island Resort
(Angaagau)
Dhekunuhau

Lily Beach Resort
(Huvahendhoo)
Huvahendhoo Kandu

Hilton Maldives
Resort & Spa
(Rangali Finolhu)
Mirihi
Island Resort
Funhau

Vilamendhoo
Island Resort
Athulivaru Falhu

Vilamendhoo Uthuru Kandu

Rangali
Gohraalhuhau
Al Kareem, 2000
Vilamendhoo Kandu
Orimas Faru

Madi-Ge,
September 21, 2000
Holhi Holhi
Ranveli Village (Viligilivaru)

Twin Island Resort
(Maafushivaru)
Dhangethi Kandu

MADIVARU
Rangali Kandu
Dhehassanu
Lonu Bui Huraa
(67m)
Dhangethi (786)

Faruhuruvalhu
Machchafushi
Island Resort
Kudhi Maa,
March 1998

Hukurudhoo Uthuru Kandu
Mirihi Maahaa
Machchafushimathi Faru

Hukurudhoo
Vakarufalhi
Island Resort
Kudarah
Island Resort

Hukurudhoo Dhekunu Kandu
KUDA RAH THILA
Dhigurashu Kandu

Huruelhi
Finolhu
Dhuvan Faru

Heygahathu Kandu
Dhonkadhdhaa Hau
Dhuvanfaruhau

Maahaa
Dhashu Rongali

Mathi Rongali
Dhigurah (520)

Rashukolhuhuraa

Medufinolhu

SOUTH ARI
ATOLL
(ALIFU DHAALU)

Bodufinolhu
Fenfushi (157)
Tholhufushi
Rhandi II,
1998
White Sands
Resort
(Dhidhdhoo Finolhu)

(1927)
Maamigili
(Proposed airport)
Dhidhdhoo (157)

Sun Island
(Nalaguraidhoo)
Kudadhoo
Hiyafushi

Holiday Island
(Dhiffushi)
Ariyadhoo
Ariyadhoo Kandu
Ariyadhoo Haitha
Maamigili Kandu

MALÉ

0   2   4   6   8   10 km
SCALE in Kilometres
WARNING : Map not to be used for navigation purposes

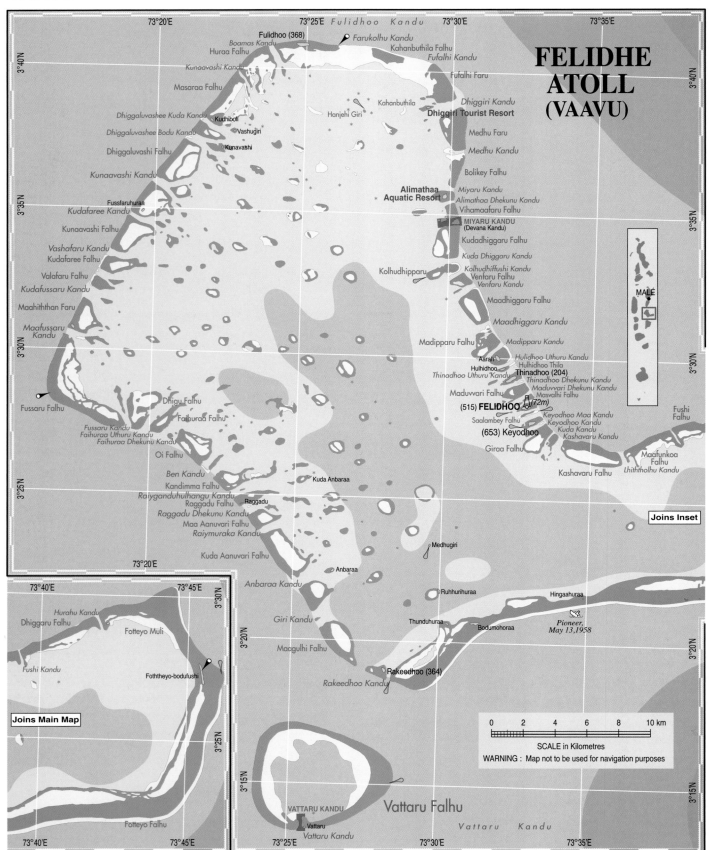

FELIDHE
ATOLL
(VAAVU)

Fulidhoo Kandu

73°20'E 73°25'E 73°30'E 73°35'E

3°40'N

Fulidhoo (368)
Boamas Kandu
Huraa Falhu
Farukolhu Kandu
Kahanbuthila Falhu
Fufalhi Kandu

Kunaavashi Kandu
Fufalhi Faru

Masaraa Falhu
Dhiggiri Kandu

Dhiggaluvashee Kuda Kandu
Kudhiboli
Hanjehi Giri
Kahanbuthila
Dhiggiri Tourist Resort

Dhiggaluvashee Bodu Kandu
Vashugiri
Medhu Faru

Dhiggaluvashi Falhu
Kunavashi
Medhu Kandu

Bolikey Falhu

3°35'N

Kunaavashi Kandu
Miyaru Kandu

Alimathaa
Aquatic Resort
Alimathaa Dhekunu Kandu

Fussfaruhuraa
Vihamaafaru Falhu

Kudafaree Kandu
MIYARU KANDU
(Devana Kandu)

Kunaavashi Falhu
Kudadhiggaru Falhu

Vashafaru Kandu
Kuda Dhiggaru Kandu

Kudafaree Falhu
Kolhudhipparu
Kolhudhiffushi Kandu
Venfaru Falhu

Valafaru Falhu
Venfaru Kandu

Kudafussaru Kandu
Maadhiggaru Falhu

Maahiththan Faru
Maadhiggaru Kandu

3°30'N

Maafussaru
Kandu
Madipparu Falhu
Madipparu Kandu

Aarah
Hulidhoo Uthuru Kandu
Hulhidhoo
Hulhidhoo Thila

Thinadhoo Uthuru Kandu
Thinadhoo (204)
Thinadhoo Dhekunu Kandu
Maduvvari Dhekunu Kandu

Dhigu Falhu
Maduvvari Falhu
Masvalhi Falhu

Fussaru Falhu
Faihuraa Falhu
(72m)
(515) FELIDHOO

Fussaru Kandu
Faihuraa Uthuru Kandu
Faihuraa Dhekunu Kandu
Saalambey Falhu
Keyodhoo Maa Kandu
Keyodhoo Kandu
Kuda Kandu

Oi Falhu
(653) Keyodhoo
Kashavaru Kandu

Giraa Falhu
Maafunkoa
Falhu

Ben Kandu
Kuda Anbaraa
Kashavaru Falhu
Lhithitholhu Kandu

Kandimma Falhu

Raiyganduhulhangu Kandu
Raggadu Falhu
Raggadu

Raggadu Dhekunu Kandu
Medhugiri

Maa Aanuvari Falhu
Raiymuraka Kandu

Kuda Aanuvari Falhu
Anbaraa

Ruhhurihuraa
Hingaahuraa

Anbaraa Kandu

Giri Kandu
Thunduhuraa
Bodumohoraa
Pioneer,
May 13,1958

Maagulhi Falhu

Rakeedhoo (364)
Rakeedhoo Kandu

Joins Inset

MALÉ

Fushi
Falhu

Inset (bottom left):

73°40'E 73°45'E

3°30'N

Hurahu Kandu
Dhiggaru Falhu
Fotteyo Muli

Fushi Kandu
Foththeyo-bodufushi

Joins Main Map

3°25'N

Fotteyo Falhu

73°40'E 73°45'E

Bottom right:

73°25'E 73°30'E 73°35'E

3°15'N

VATTARU KANDU
Vattaru
Vattaru Falhu
Vattaru Kandu
Vattaru Kandu

0 2 4 6 8 10 km

SCALE in Kilometres
WARNING : Map not to be used for navigation purposes

MAP 14

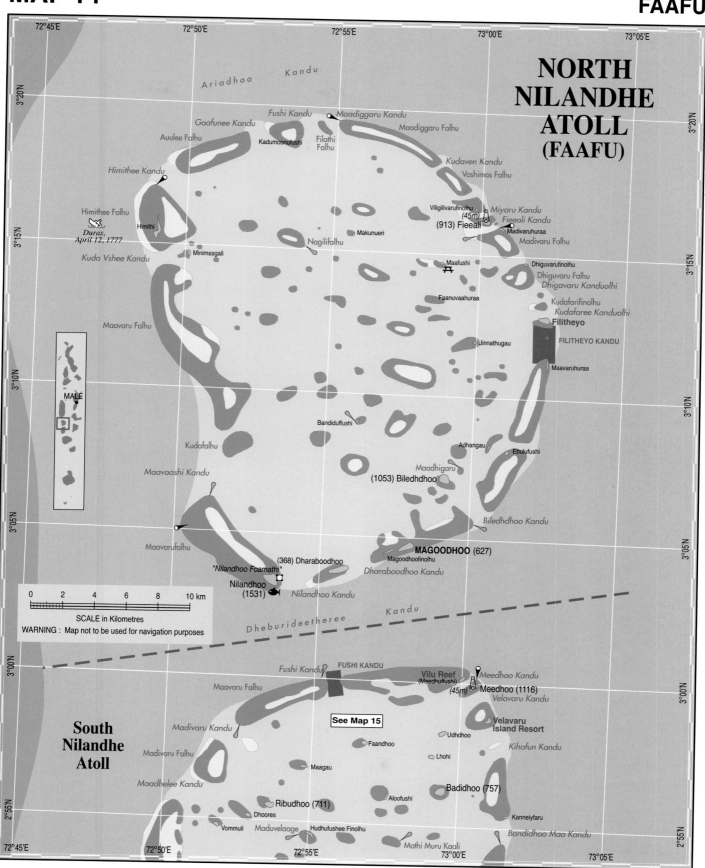

NORTH NILANDHE ATOLL (FAAFU)

Ariadhoo   Kandu

Gaafunee Kandu

Fushi Kandu   Maadiggaru Kandu

Auulee Falhu   Kadumoonufushi   *Maadiggaru Falhu*

Filathi Falhu

Himithee Kandu   *Kudaven Kandu*

Voshimas Falhu

Himithee Falhu   Viligilivarufinolhu   *Miyaru Kandu*

(45m)   *Fieeali Kandu*

Himithi   (913) Fieeali   Madivaruhuraa

Duras, April 12, 1777   Makunueri   *Madivaru Falhu*

Kuda Vshee Kandu   *Nagilifalhu*

Minimasgali   Dhiguvarufinolhu

Dhiguvaru Falhu

Maafushi   *Dhigavaru Kanduolhi*

Kudafarifinolhu

Kudafaree Kanduolhi

Faanuvaahuraa   **Filitheyo**

Maavaru Falhu   Jinnathugau   FILITHEYO KANDU

Maavaruhuraa

MALÉ   Bandiduffushi   Adhangau

Ebulufushi

Kudafalhu   *Maadhigaru*

Maavaashi Kandu   (1053) Biledhdhoo

Biledhdhoo Kandu

Maavarufalhu   MAGOODHOO (627)

Magoodhoofinolhu

(368) Dharaboodhoo   *Dharaboodhoo Kandu*

"Nilandhoo Foamathi"

Nilandhoo (1531)   *Nilandhoo Kandu*

Dheburideetheree   Kandu

| 0 | 2 | 4 | 6 | 8 | 10 km |

SCALE in Kilometres

WARNING : Map not to be used for navigation purposes

Fushi Kandu   FUSHI KANDU

Maavaru Falhu   Vilu Reef   *Meedhoo Kandu*

(Meedhuffushi)

(45m)   Meedhoo (1116)

South Nilandhe Atoll   *Velavaru Kandu*

Madivaru Kandu   **See Map 15**   **Velavaru Island Resort**

Madivaru Falhu   Udhdhoo

Kihafun Kandu

Faandhoo

Maadhelee Kandu   Lhohi

Maagau

Badidhoo (757)

Ribudhoo (711)   Aloofushi

Dhoores   Kanneiyfaru

Vommuli   Maduvelaage   Hudhufushee Finolhu

Mathi Muru Kaali   *Bandidhoo Maa Kandu*

MAP 15

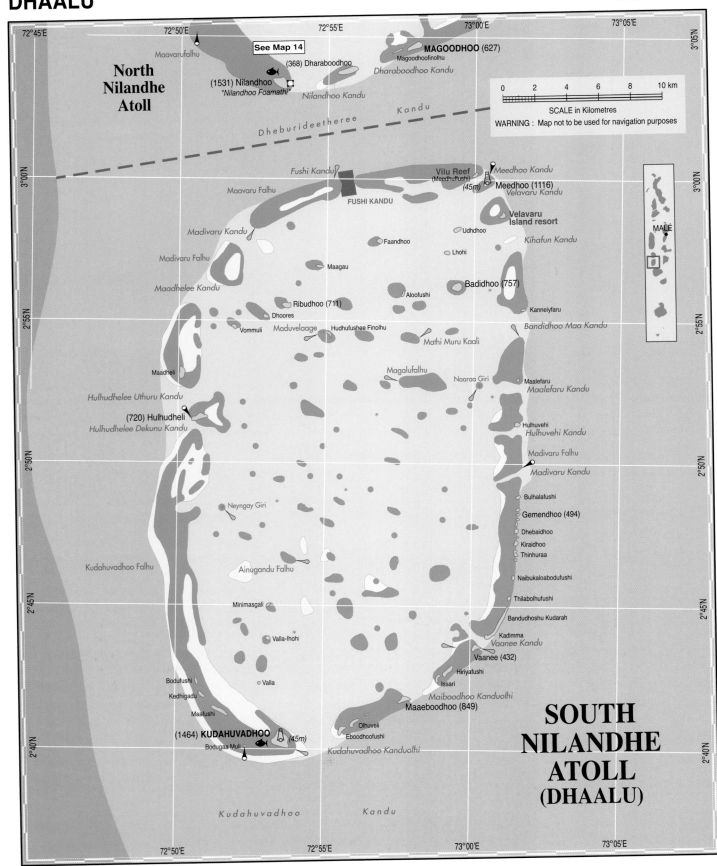

North Nilandhe Atoll

Maavarufalhu

See Map 14

(368) Dharaboodhoo

MAGOODHOO (627)

Magoodhoofinolhu

(1531) Nilandhoo
"Nilandhoo Foamathi"

Dharaboodhoo Kandu

Nilandhoo Kandu

Dheburideetheree *Kandu*

| 0 | 2 | 4 | 6 | 8 | 10 km |

SCALE in Kilometres

WARNING : Map not to be used for navigation purposes

Fushi Kandu

Vilu Reef
(Meedhuffushi)

Meedhoo Kandu

Maavaru Falhu

(45m)

Meedhoo (1116)

Velavaru Kandu

FUSHI KANDU

Madivaru Kandu

Velavaru Island resort

Madivaru Falhu

Faandhoo

Udhdhoo

Kihafun Kandu

Lhohi

Maadhelee Kandu

Maagau

Badidhoo (757)

Aloofushi

Ribudhoo (711)

Kanneiyfaru

Dhoores

Bandidhoo Maa Kandu

Vommuli

Maduvelaage

Hudhufushee Finolhu

Mathi Muru Kaali

Maadheli

Magalufalhu

Naaraa Giri

Maalefaru

Maalefaru Kandu

Hulhudhelee Uthuru Kandu

(720) Hulhudheli

Hulhuvehi

Hulhudhelee Dekunu Kandu

Hulhuvehi Kandu

Madivaru Falhu

Madivaru Kandu

Bulhalafushi

Gemendhoo (494)

Neyngay Giri

Dhebaidhoo

Kiraidhoo

Thinhuraa

Kudahuvadhoo Falhu

Ainugandu Falhu

Naibukaloabodufushi

Thilabolhufushi

Minimasgali

Bandudhoshu Kudarah

Kadimma

Vaanee Kandu

Valla-Ihohi

Vaanee (432)

Hiriyafushi

Bodufushi

Valla

Issari

Maiboodhoo Kanduolhi

Kedhigadu

Maaeeboodhoo (849)

Maafushi

Olhuveli

SOUTH NILANDHE ATOLL (DHAALU)

(1464) **KUDAHUVADHOO**

(45m)

Eboodhoofushi

Bodugaa Muli

Kudahuvadhoo Kanduolhi

Kudahuvadhoo *Kandu*

MALÉ

MAP 16

MEEMU

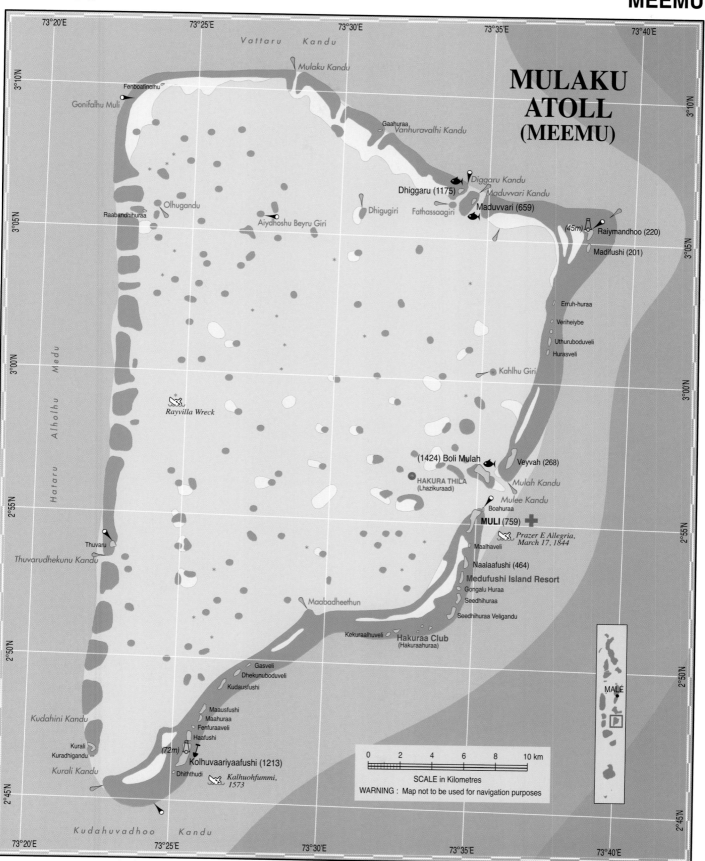

MULAKU ATOLL (MEEMU)

Vattaru Kandu

Mulaku Kandu

Fenboafinolhu

Gonifalhu Muli

Gaahuraa
Vanhuravalhi Kandu

Diggaru Kandu
Dhiggaru (1175)
Maduvvari Kandu

Raabandhihuraa
Olhugandu

Dhigugiri
Fathassaagiri
Maduvvari (659)

Aiydhoshu Beyru Giri

(45m)
Raiymandhoo (220)

Madifushi (201)

Erruh-huraa

Veriheiybe

Uthuruboduveli

Hurasveli

Kahlhu Giri

Rayvilla Wreck

(1424) Boli Mulah

Veyvah (268)

Mulah Kandu

HAKURA THILA
(Lhazikuraadi)

Mulee Kandu
Boahuraa

MULI (759) ✚

Prazer E Allegria,
March 17, 1844

Thuvaru

Thuvarudhekunu Kandu

Maalhaveli

Naalaafushi (464)

Medufushi Island Resort
Gongalu Huraa
Seedhihuraa
Seedhihuraa Veligandu

Maabadheethun

Kekuraalhuveli
Hakuraa Club
(Hakuraahuraa)

Gasveli
Dhekunuboduveli
Kudausfushi

Maausfushi
Maahuraa
Fenfuraaveli
Haafushi

Kurali
Kuradhigandu

(72m)
Kolhuvaariyaafushi (1213)

Kurali Kandu

Dhiththudi
Kalhuohfummi,
1573

Kudahini Kandu

Kudahuvadhoo Kandu

Hataru Alholhu Medu

MALE

| 0 | 2 | 4 | 6 | 8 | 10 km |

SCALE in Kilometres
WARNING : Map not to be used for navigation purposes

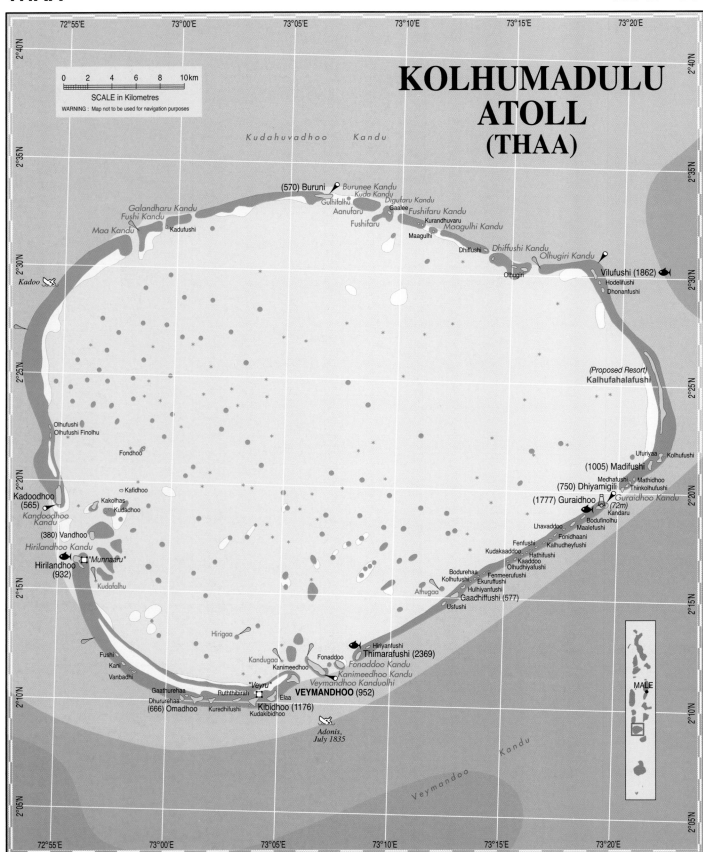

KOLHUMADULU ATOLL (THAA)

Kudahuvadhoo　Kandu

(570) Buruni
Burunee Kandu
Kuda Kandu
Gulhifalhu
Digufaru Kandu
Aanufaru
Gaalee
Fushifaru Kandu
Fushifaru
Kurandhuvaru
Maagulhi Kandu
Maagulhi

Galandharu Kandu
Fushi Kandu
Kadufushi
Maa Kandu

Dhiffushi
Dhiffushi Kandu
Olhugiri
Olhugiri Kandu
Vilufushi (1862)

Kadoo

Hodelifushi
Dhonanfushi

(Proposed Resort)
Kalhufahalafushi

Olhufushi
Olhufushi Finolhu

Fondhoo

Ufuriyaa　Kolhufushi

(1005) Madifushi
Medhafushi　Mathidhoo
(750) Dhiyamigili　Thinkolhufushi
(1777) Guraidhoo　*Guraidhoo Kandu*
Kadoodhoo
(565)
Kandoodhoo Kandu
Kafidhoo
Kakolhas
Kudadhoo
Kandaru
Bodufinolhu
Lhavaddoo
Fonidhaani
(380) Vandhoo
Maalefushi
Hirilandhoo Kandu
Fenfushi　Kalhudheyfushi
Kudakaaddoo　Hathifushi
Hirilandhoo
(932)
□ "*Munnaaru*"
Kaaddoo
Olhudhiyafushi
Kudafalhu
Bodurehaa　Fenmeerufushi
Kolhufushi　Ekuruffushi
Hulhiyanfushi
Athugaa
Gaadhiffushi (577)
Usfushi
Hirigaa

Fushi
Kani
Vanbadhi
Gaathurehaa
Dhururehaa
(666) Omadhoo
Kandugaa
Kanimeedhoo
Fonaddoo
Hiriyanfushi
Thimarafushi (2369)
Fonaddoo Kandu
Kanimeedhoo Kandu
"*Veyru*"
Ruththibirah
Elaa
Veymandhoo Kanduolhi
VEYMANDHOO (952)
Kudakibidhoo
Kibidhoo (1176)
Kuredhifushi

Adonis,
July 1835

Veymandoo　*Kandu*

MALE

MAP 18

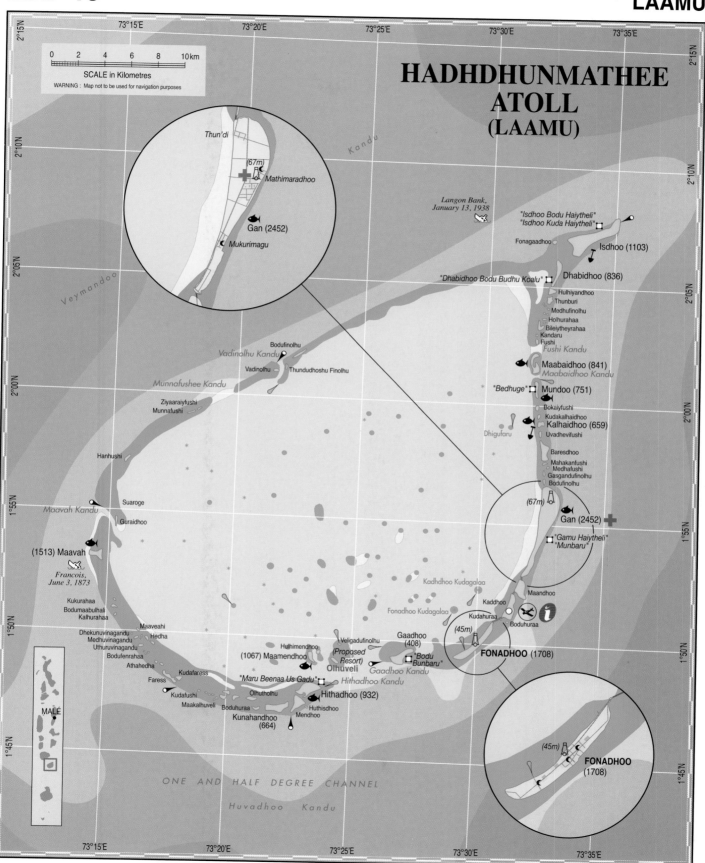

HADHDHUNMATHEE ATOLL (LAAMU)

0 2 4 6 8 10km
SCALE in Kilometres
WARNING : Map not to be used for navigation purposes

Thun'di

(67m)
Mathimaradhoo
Gan (2452)
Mukurimagu

Kandu

*Langon Bank,
January 13, 1938*

"Isdhoo Bodu Haiytheli"
"Isdhoo Kuda Haiytheli"
Fonagaadhoo
Isdhoo (1103)

"Dhabidhoo Bodu Budhu Koalu"
Dhabidhoo (836)

Hulhiyandhoo
Thunburi
Medhufinolhu
Holhurahaa
Bileiytheyrahaa
Kandaru
Fushi
Fushi Kandu

Maabaidhoo (841)
Maabaidhoo Kandu

"Bedhuge"
Mundoo (751)

Bokaiyfushi
Kudakalhaidhoo
Kalhaidhoo (659)
Uvadhevifushi

Dhigufaru

Baresdhoo
Mahakanfushi
Medhafushi
Gasgandufinolhu
Bodufinolhu

(67m)
Gan (2452)

"Gamu Haiytheli"
"Munbaru"

Bodufinolhu
Vadinolhu Kandu

Veymandoo

Vadinolhu
Thundudhoshu Finolhu

Munnafushee Kandu

Ziyaaraiyfushi
Munnafushi

Hanhushi

Suaroge
Maavah Kandu
Guraidhoo

(1513) Maavah

*Francois,
June 3, 1873*

Kukurahaa
Bodumaabulhali
Kalhurahaa

Maaveahi
Hedha

Dhekunuvinagandu
Medhuvinagandu
Uthuruvinagandu
Bodufenrahaa
Athahedha
Kudafaress
Faress
Kudafushi
Maakalhuveli

Hulhimendhoo
(1067) Maamendhoo

Veligadufinolhu
(Proposed Resort)
Olhuveli

"Maru Beenaa Us Gadu"
Olhutholhu
Boduhuraa
Kunahandhoo
(664)
Huthisdhoo
Mendhoo

Hithadhoo (932)

Hithadhoo Kandu

Gaadhoo (408)
"Bodu Bunbaru"
Gaadhoo Kandu

Kadhdhoo Kudagalaa

Fonadhoo Kudagalaa
Kaddhoo
Kudahuraa
(45m)
Boduhuraa
FONADHOO (1708)

Maandhoo

MALÉ

ONE AND HALF DEGREE CHANNEL

Huvadhoo Kandu

(45m)
FONADHOO
(1708)

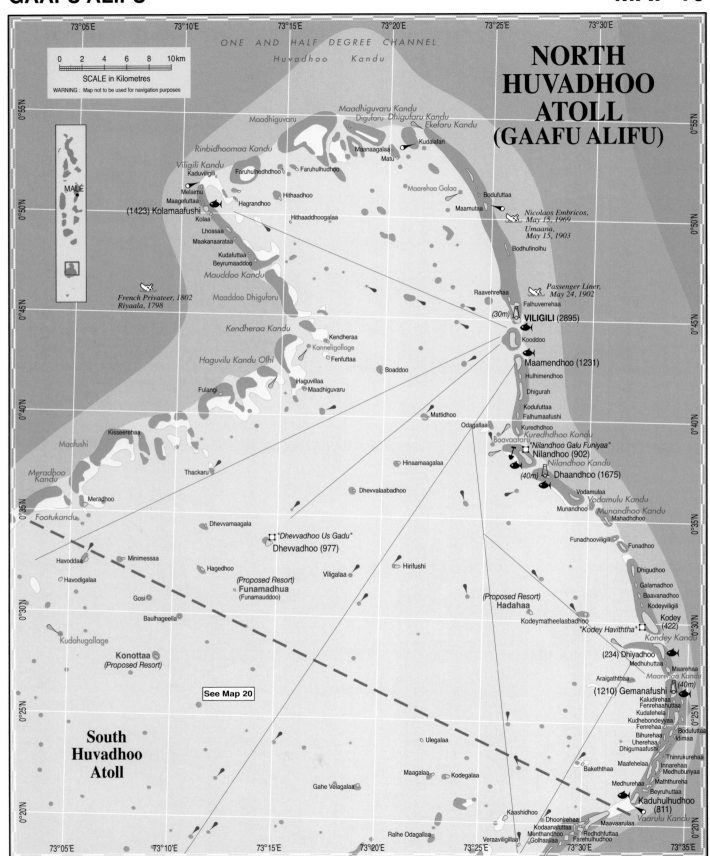

ONE AND HALF DEGREE CHANNEL
Huvadhoo Kandu

NORTH HUVADHOO ATOLL (GAAFU ALIFU)

0   2   4   6   8   10km
SCALE in Kilometres
WARNING : Map not to be used for navigation purposes

MALÉ

Maadhiguvaru Kandu
Maadhiguvaru   Digufaru   Dhigufaru Kandu
                                    Ekefaru Kandu
Rinbidhoomaa Kandu   Kudalafari
                            Maanaagalaa
Viligili Kandu   Matu
Kaduviligili   Faruhulhedhdhoo   Faruhulhudhoo
Melaimu   Maarehaa Galaa   Bodufuttaa
Maagefuttaa   Hithaadhoo   Maamutaa
(1423) Kolamaafushi   Hagrandhoo   *Nicolaos Embricos,*
Kolaa   *May 15, 1969*
Lhossaa   Hithaaddhoogalaa   *Umaana,*
Maakanaarataa   *May 15, 1903*
Kudafuttaa   Bodhufinolhu
Beyrumaaddoo
Mauddoo Kandu
Maaddoo Dhigufaru   Raavehrehaa   *Passenger Liner,*
French Privateer, 1802   Falhuverrehaa *May 24, 1902*
Riyaala, 1798   **(30m)**
Kendheraa Kandu   **VILIGILI (2895)**
                                    Kendheraa   Kooddoo
Haguvilu Kandu Olhi   Kanneligallage   **Maamendhoo (1231)**
                                    Fenfuttaa   Hulhimendhoo
                        Boaddoo   Dhigurah
Fulangi   Haguvillaa   Kodufuttaa
               Maadhiguvaru   Falhumaafushi
                                                       Kuredhdhoo
                                       Mattidhoo   Odagallaa *Kuredhdhoo Kandu*
                                                       Boavaataru
Kisseerehaa   "Nilandhoo Galu Funiyaa"
Maafushi   Hinaamaagalaa   **Nilandhoo (902)**
                                                       Nilandhoo Kandu
Meradhoo   Thackaru   **(40m)** **Dhaandhoo (1675)**
Kandu   Vodamulaa
Meradhoo   Dhevvalaabadhoo   *Vodamulu Kandu*
Footukandu   Munandhoo *Munandhoo Kandu*
                                                       Mahadhdhoo
                    Dhevvamaagala
                                                       Funadhooviligili   Funadhoo
Havoddaa   Minimessaa   "Dhevvadhoo Us Gadu"
                            Dhevvadhoo (977)   Dhigudhoo
Havodigalaa   Hagedhoo   Galamadhoo
Gosi   Viligalaa   Baavanadhoo
                    (Proposed Resort)   Hirifushi Kodeyviligili
Baulhageella   **Funamadhua**   **Kodey**
                    (Funamauddoo)   *(Proposed Resort)* **(422)**
Kudahugallage   **Hadahaa**   "Kodey Haviththa"
                                    Kodeymatheelaabadhoo *Kondey Kandu*
Konottaa   **(234) Dhiyadhoo**
(Proposed Resort)   Medhuhuttaa
                                                                  Maarehaa
See Map 20   Araigaththaa   **(40m)**
                                                      (1210) Gemanafushi *Maarehaa Kandu*
                                                      Kaludirehaa
                                                      Fenrehaahuttaa
South Huvadhoo Atoll   Kudafehela
                                                      Kudhebondeyyda
                                                      Fenrehaa   Boduffutaa
                                                      Bihurehaa   Idimaa
                                                      Uherehaa
                                                      Dhigumaafushi
                            Ulegalaa   Maafehelaa   Thinrukurehaa
                                                                   Innarehaa
                                                      Bakeththaa   Medhuburiyaa
                                                                   Maththureha
                                    Maagalaa   Medhurehaa   Beyruhuttaa
                       Gahe Velagalaa   Kodegalaa   **Kaduhulhudhoo**
                                                                   (811)
                                                      Kodaanafuttaa *Vaarulu Kandu*
                            Kaashidhoo   Dhoonirehaa Maavaarulaa
             Ralhe Odagallaa   Menthandhoo Redhdhuttaa
                                    Veraaviligillaa Golhaalaa Farehulhudhoo

MAP 20

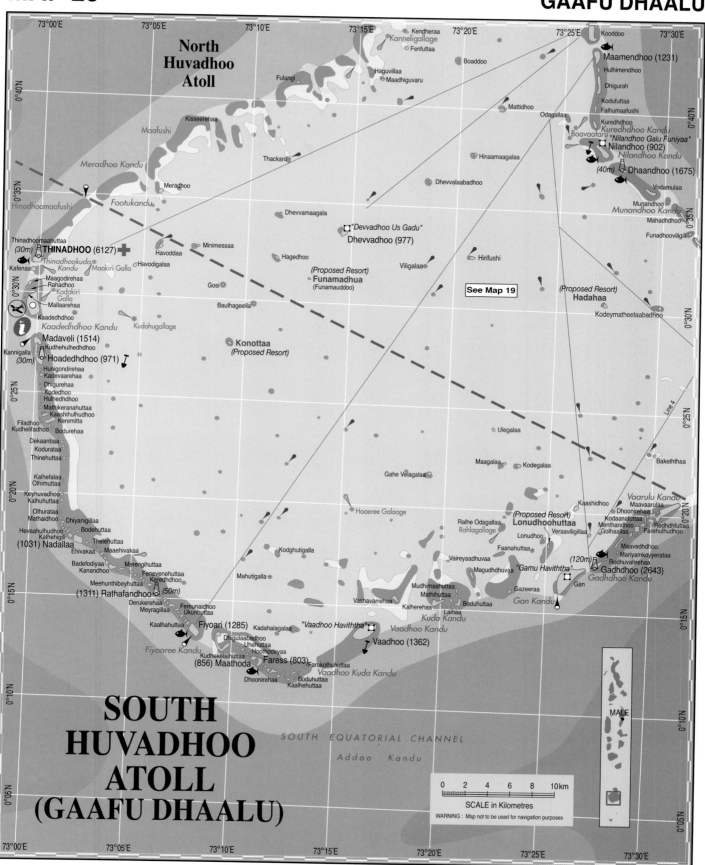

**North
Huvadhoo
Atoll**

73°00'E 73°05'E 73°10'E 73°15'E 73°20'E 73°25'E 73°30'E

Kendheraa
Kanneligallage
Kooddoo
Fenfuttaa
Boaddoo
Maamendhoo (1231)
Fulangi
Haguvillaa
Hulhimendhoo
Maadhiguvaru
Dhigurah
Mattidhoo
Kodufuttaa
Falhumaafushi
Kisseerehaa
Odagallaa
Kuredhdhoo
Maafushi
Kuredhdhoo Kandu
Boavaataru
"Nilandhoo Galu Funiyaa"
Hinaamaagalaa
Nilandhoo (902)
Thackaru
Nilandhoo Kandu
Meradhoo Kandu
(40m)
Dhaandhoo (1675)
Meradhoo
Dhevvalaabadhoo
Vodamulaa
Footukandu
Munandhoo
Mahadhdhoo
Munandhoo Kandu
Hinadhoomaafushi
Dhevvamaagala
Funadhooviligilli
"Devvadhoo Us Gadu"
Thinadhoomaahuttaa
Dhevvadhoo (977)
(30m) **THINADHOO (6127)**
Havoddaa
Minimessaa
Thinadhookuda
Hagedhoo
Hirifushi
Kafenaa
Kandu
Havodigalaa
Viligalaa
Maagodirehaa
Maakiri Galla
(Proposed Resort)
Rahadhoo
Gosi
Funamadhua
Kodakiri
(Funamauddoo)
Galla
Mallaarehaa
(Proposed Resort)
Kaadedhdhoo
Baulhageella
Hadahaa
Kaadedhdhoo Kandu
Kudahugallage
Kodeymatheelaabadhoo
See Map 19
Madaveli (1514)
Konottaa
Kudhehulhedhdhoo
(Proposed Resort)
Hoadedhdhoo (971)
Kannigalla
(30m)
Hunigondirehaa
Kadevaarehaa
Dhigurehaa
Kodedhoo
Hulhedhdhoo
Ulegalaa
Mathikeranahuttaa
Kaashihulhudhoo
Keremitta
Filadhoo
Kudhelifadhoo
Bodurehaa
Dekaanbaa
Kodurataa
Thinehuttaa
Maagalaa
Kodegalaa
Bakeththaa
Kalhefalaa
Olhimuttaa
Gahe Velagalaa
Keyhuvadhoo
Kalhuhuttaa
Olhurataa
Vaarulu Kandu
Mathaidhoo
Dhiyanigillaa
Kaashidhoo
Maavaarulaa
Hevaahulhudhoo
Bodehuttaa
Haaeree Galaage
(Proposed Resort)
Dhoonirehaa
Kalhehigili
Thelehuttaa
Ralhe Odagallaa
Lonudhoohuttaa
Kodaanahuttaa
(1031) Nadallaa
Maaehivakaa
Rahlagallage
Menthandhoo
Redhdhfuttaa
Ehivakaa
Veraaviligillaa
Golhaallaa
Farehulhudhoo
Badefodiyaa
Morengihuttaa
Kodghutigalla
Lonudhoo
Kanandhoo
Maavedhdhoo
Meehunthibeyhuttaa
Fenevenehuttaa
Vaireyaadhuvaa
Faanahuttaa
(120m)
Mariyamkoyyerataa
(1311) Rathafandhoo
Keredhdhoo
Mahutigalla
Vashavarrehaa
Magudhdhuvaa
"Gamu Haviththa"
Roduvarehaa
(50m)
Gadhdhoo (2643)
Derukerehaa
Femunaidhoo
Mudhimaahuttaa
Gan
Gadhdhoo Kandu
Meyragillaa
Ukunhuttaa
Mathihuttaa
Gazeeraa
Kaalhahuttaa
Fiyoari (1285)
Kadahalagalaa
Kalherehaa
Laihaa
Boduhuttaa
Gan Kandu
"Vaadhoo Haviththa"
Dhigulaabadhoo
Kudo Kandu
Fiyoaree Kandu
Uhehuttaa
Vaadhoo Kandu
Kudhekelaihuttaa
Hoothodeyaa
Vaadhoo (1362)
(856) Maathoda
Faress (803)
Farukolhuhuttaa
Dhoonirehaa
Boduhuttaa
Vaadhoo Kuda Kandu
Kaalhehuttaa

SOUTH
HUVADHOO
ATOLL
(GAAFU DHAALU)

SOUTH EQUATORIAL CHANNEL

Addoo Kandu

0°40'N
0°35'N
0°30'N
0°25'N
0°20'N
0°15'N
0°10'N
0°05'N

MALE

0 2 4 6 8 10km
SCALE in Kilometres
WARNING : Map not to be used for navigation purposes

73°00'E 73°05'E 73°10'E 73°15'E 73°20'E 73°25'E 73°30'E

Photo courtesy Sigurd Schjoett

1 The island of Foammulah, showing the 120 meter communications tower.

2 New Harbour in Foammulah.

3 In the past, goods were landed by small dhoani on the beach at Foammulah.

4 Old Mosque on Foammulah.

Photo courtesy Ahmed Nazim

MAP 21

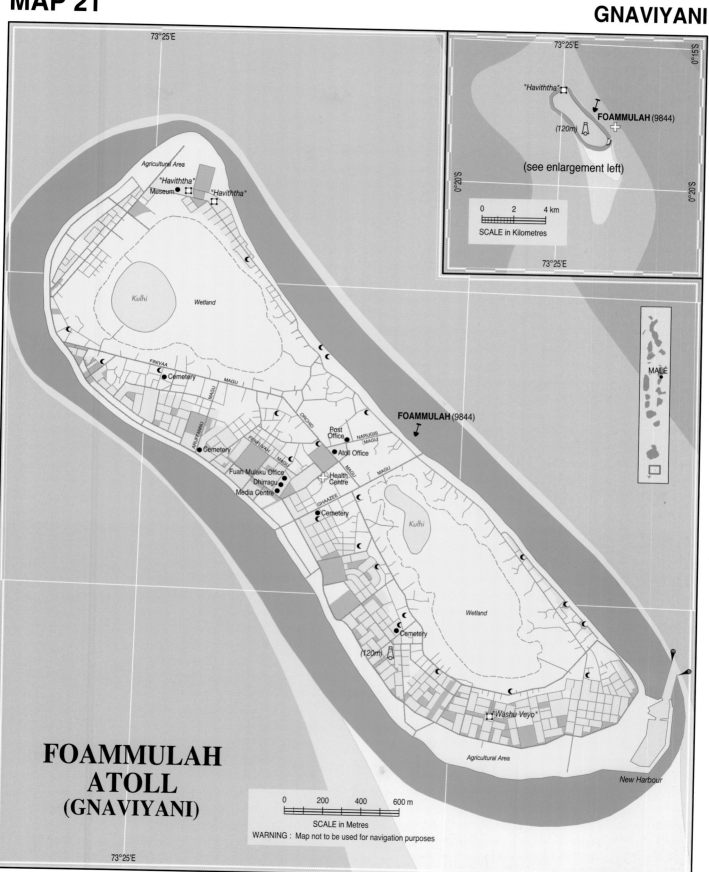

73°25'E

"Haviththa"

FOAMMULAH (9844)

(120m)

(see enlargement left)

0 2 4 km

SCALE in Kilometres

73°25'E

0°15'S

0°20'S

0°20'S

Agricultural Area

"Haviththa"
Museum ● □ □ "Haviththa"

Kulhi

Wetland

MALÉ

FINIVAA

MAGU

● Cemetery

MAGU

ORCHID

ARUFFANNU

FENFUVAH

MAGU

● Cemetery

Post
Office

NARUGIS
MAGU

● Atoll Office

FOAMMULAH (9844)

Fuah Mulaku Office
Dhirragu ●
Media Centre ●

Health
Centre

MAGU

MAGU

GHAAZEE

● Cemetery

Kulhi

Wetland

● Cemetery

(120m)

"Washu Veyo" □

Agricultural Area

New Harbour

FOAMMULAH
ATOLL
(GNAVIYANI)

0 200 400 600 m

SCALE in Metres

WARNING : Map not to be used for navigation purposes

73°25'E

45

1 The regional airport of Kaadedhdhoo, Gaafu Dhaalu.   **2** British War memorial on Gan, Seenu.
3 Eidhigali Kulhi on Hithadhoo, Seenu.   **4** Propeller of the British Loyalty, Seenu.
5 Remains of a World War II submarine net, Viligili Kandu, Seenu

MAP 22

SEENU

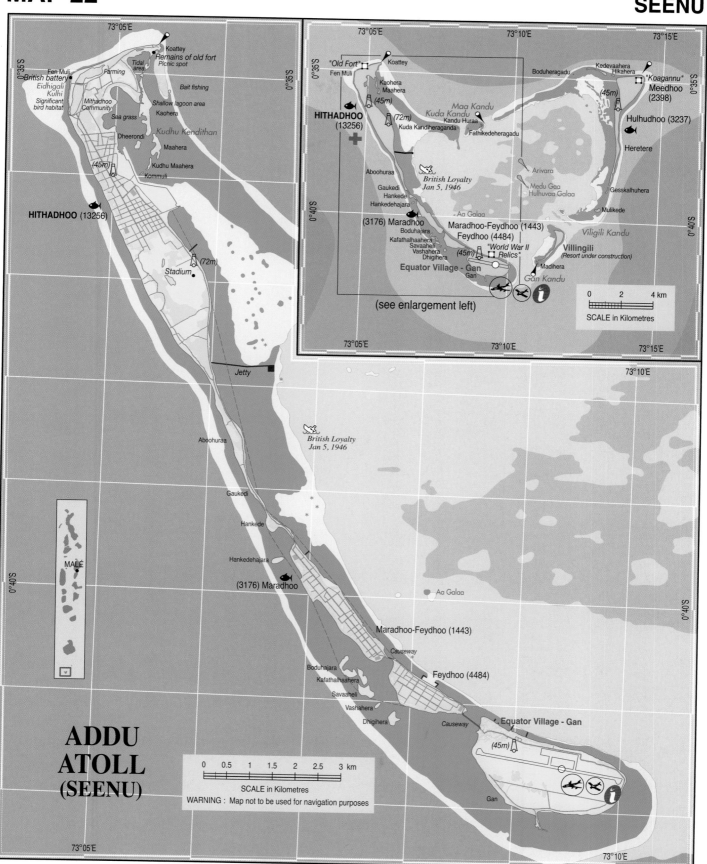

MAP 22 — SEENU

73°05'E

Koattey
Remains of old fort
Picnic spot
Fen Muli
British battery
Eidhigali Kulhi
Significant bird habitat
Tidal area
Farming
Mithadhoo Community
Sea grass
Bait fishing
Shallow lagoon area
Kaohera

Kudhu Kendithan

Dheerondi
Maahera
Kudhu Maahera
Kommuli
(45m)

HITHADHOO (13256)

(72m)
Stadium

Jetty

Aboohuraa

British Loyalty
Jan 5, 1946

Gaukedi
Hankede
Hankedehajara

(3176) Maradhoo

Aa Galaa

Maradhoo-Feydhoo (1443)
Causeway
Boduhajara
Kafathalhaahera
Savaaheli
Vashahera
Dhigihera
Feydhoo (4484)
Causeway
Equator Village - Gan
(45m)
Gan

MALÉ

ADDU ATOLL (SEENU)

0   0.5   1   1.5   2   2.5   3 km
SCALE in Kilometres
WARNING : Map not to be used for navigation purposes

73°05'E   73°10'E   73°15'E

"Old Fort"
Koattey
Fen Muli
Kaohera
Maahera
(45m)
HITHADHOO (13256)
(72m)
Kuda Kandiheraganda
Maa Kandu
Kuda Kandu
Kandu Huraa
Fathikedeheragadu
Boduheragadu
Kedevaahera
Hikahera
"Koagannu"
Meedhoo (2398)
(45m)
Hulhudhoo (3237)
Heretere
British Loyalty, Jan 5, 1946
Arivara
Medu Gaa
Hulhuvaa Galaa
Gesskaluhera
Aboohuraa
Mulikede
Gaukedi
Hankede
Hankedehajara
(3176) Maradhoo
Boduhajara
Kafathalhaahera
Savaaheli
Vashahera
Dhigihera
Maradhoo-Feydhoo (1443)
Feydhoo (4484)
"World War II Relics"
(45m)
Equator Village - Gan
Gan
Madihera
Villingili (Resort under construction)
Viligili Kandu
Gan Kandu

(see enlargement left)

0   2   4 km
SCALE in Kilometres

INDEX

ISLAND NAME	ATOLL	MAP #	REFERENCE		ISLAND NAME	ATOLL	MAP #	REFERENCE	
Aarah (U)	Kaafu	9	4°14'N	73°29'E	Bodhufinolhu (U)	Gaafu Alifu	19	0°49'N	73°26'E
Aarah (U)	Raa	6	5°27'N	72°57'E	Bodubados (U)	Kaafu	9	4°17'N	73°29'E
Aarah (U)	Vaavu	13	3°30'N	73°32'E	Bodufaahuraa (U)	Lhaviyani	8	5°19'N	73°39'E
Aboohuraa (U)	Seenu	21	0°38'S	73°06'E	Bodufarufinolhu (U)	Raa	6	5°31'N	72°48'E
Adhangau (U)	Faafu	14	3°08'N	73°01'E	Bodufenmaaeboodhoo (U)	Raa	6	5°38'N	72°56'E
Adonis (Wk)	Thaa	17	2°10'N	73°12'E	Bodufenrahaa (U)	Laamu	18	1°49'N	73°17'E
Agolhitheemu (I)	Raa	6	5°48'N	73°01'E	Bodufinolhu (U)	Alifu Dhaalu	12	3°29'N	72°47'E
Ahivahfushi (U)	Baa	7	5°14'N	72°52'E	Bodufinolhu (U)	Baa	7	5°01'N	72°52'E
Aidhoo (U)	Baa	7	5°12'N	73°10'E	Bodufinolhu (U)	Kaafu	10	3°52'N	73°28'E
Akirifushi (U)	Kaafu	9	4°38'N	73°29'E	Bodufinolhu (U)	Laamu	18	2°02'N	73°23'E
Alidhoo (PR)	Haa Alifu	1	6°52'N	73°09'E	Bodufinolhu (U)	Laamu	18	1°57'N	73°33'E
Alidhuffarufinolhu (U)	Haa Alifu	1	6°52'N	73°06'E	Bodufinolhu (U)	Thaa	17	2°19'N	73°18'E
Alifushi (I)	Raa	6	5°57'N	72°57'E	Bodufolhudhoo (I)	Alifu Alifu	11	4°11'N	72°47'E
Aligau (U)	Lhaviyani	8	5°15'N	73°31'E	Bodufushi (U)	Dhaalu	15	2°43'N	72°51'E
Alikoirah (U)	Alifu Alifu	11	3°57'N	72°53'E	Bodufushi (U)	Noonu	5	5°43'N	73°25'E
Alimathaa (R)	Vaavu	13	3°36'N	73°29'E	Bodufushi (U)	Raa	6	5°31'N	72°58'E
Aloofushi (U)	Dhaalu	15	2°56'N	72°58'E	Bodufuttaa (U)	Gaafu Alifu	19	0°51'N	73°24'E
Al Kareem (Wk)	Alifu Dhaalu	12	3°37'N	72°58'E	Bodufuttaa (U)	Gaafu Alifu	19	0°25'N	73°35'E
Anbaraa (U)	Vaavu	13	3°23'N	73°26'E	Bodugaa Muli (U)	Dhaalu	15	2°40'N	72°52'E
Angaagau (U)	Alifu Dhaalu	12	3°39'N	72°49'E	Bodugaahuraa (U)	Lhaviyani	8	5°22'N	73°39'E
Angaga (R)	Alifu Dhaalu	12	3°39'N	72°49'E	Boduhaiykodi (U)	Raa	6	5°37'N	72°59'E
Anhenunfushi (U)	Baa	7	5°21'N	72°58'E	Boduhajara (U)	Seenu	21	0°41'S	73°07'E
Angsana (R)	Kaafu	9	4°18'N	73°25'E	Boduheragadu (U)	Seenu	21	0°35'S	73°12'E
Aracan (Wk)	Kaafu	9	4°45'N	73°35'E	Boduhithi (R)	Kaafu	9	4°26'N	73°23'E
Araigaththaa (U)	Gaafu Alifu	19	0°27'N	73°32'E	Boduhuraa (I)	Raa	6	5°26'N	73°0'E
Arilundhoo (U)	Raa	6	5°39'N	72°58'E	Boduhuraa (U)	Kaafu	10	3°58'N	73°31'E
Ariyadhoo (U)	Alifu Dhaalu	12	3°28'N	72°52'E	Boduhuraa (U)	Laamu	18	1°47'N	73°21'E
Asdhoo (U)	Kaafu	9	4°28'N	73°39'E	Boduhuraa (U)	Laamu	18	1°51'N	73°32'E
Asdu (R)	Kaafu	9	4°28'N	73°39'E	Bodhuhuraa (U)	Lhaviyani	8	5°24'N	73°39'E
Athahedha (U)	Laamu	18	1°48'N	73°17'E	Boduhuttaa (U)	Gaafu Dhaalu	20	0°12'N	73°13'E
Athurugau (R)	Alifu Dhaalu	12	3°53'N	72°49'E	Boduhuttaa (U)	Gaafu Dhaalu	20	0°15'N	73°21'E
Baarah (I)	Haa Alifu	1	6°49'N	73°12'E	Bodukaashihuraa (U)	Alifu Dhaalu	12	3°53'N	72°58'E
Baavanadhoo (U)	Gaafu Alifu	19	0°32'N	73°32'E	Bodulhaimendhoo (U)	Noonu	5	6°00'N	73°18'E
Badaidhidhdhoo (U)	Noonu	5	5°41'N	73°16'E	Bodumaabulhali (U)	Laamu	18	1°51'N	73°16'E
Badaveri (U)	Raa	6	5°37'N	72°52'E	Bodumohoraa (U)	Vaavu	13	3°21'N	73°32'E
Badefodiyaa (U)	Gaafu Dhaalu	20	0°17'N	73°04'E	Bodunaagoashi (U)	Haa Dhaalu	3	6°40'N	72°53'E
Badidhoo (I)	Dhaalu	15	2°56'N	72°59'E	Bodurehaa (U)	Gaafu Dhaalu	20	0°23'N	73°01'E
Bahurukabeeru (U)	Lhaviyani	8	5°23'N	73°24'E	Bodurehaa (U)	Thaa	17	2°16'N	73°14'E
Bakeththaa (U)	Gaafu Alifu	19	0°23'N	73°30'E	Boifushi (U)	Baa	7	5°18'N	72°59'E
Banana Reef (P)	Kaafu	9	4°15'N	73°32'E	Bokaiyfushi (U)	Laamu	18	2°00'N	73°32'E
Bandiduffushi (U)	Faafu	14	3°09'N	72°56'E	Boli Mulah (I)	Meemu	16	2°57'N	73°35'E
Bandos (R)	Kaafu	9	4°17'N	73°29'E	Bolifushi (R)	Kaafu	10	4°06'N	73°24'E
Bandudhoshu Kudarah (U)	Dhaalu	15	2°45'N	73°02'E	Bolifushi (Wk)	Kaafu	10	4°06'N	73°24'E
Banyan Tree (R)	Kaafu	9	4°18'N	73°26'E	Bomasdhoo (U)	Noonu	5	5°58'N	73°21'E
Baresdhoo (U)	Laamu	18	1°58'N	73°33'E	British Loyalty (Wk)	Seenu	21	0°42'S	73°07'E
Baros (R)	Kaafu	9	4°17'N	73°26'E	Bulhaalhohi (U)	Alifu Dhaalu	12	3°44'N	72°44'E
Bathala (R)	Alifu Alifu	11	4°04'N	72°58'E	Bulhalafushi (U)	Dhaalu	15	2°49'N	73°02'E
Bathalaa (U)	Baa	7	5°22'N	73°04'E	Burehifasdhoo (U)	Noonu	5	5°58'N	73°22'E
Baulhageella (U)	Gaafu Dhaalu	20	0°30'N	73°10'E	Buruni (I)	Thaa	17	2°34'N	73°06'E
Beenaafushi (U)	Haa Alifu	1	6°56'N	73°08'E	Captain Pentalis (Wk)	Haa Alifu	1	6°53'N	73°14'E
Berimmadhoo (I)	Haa Alifu	1	7°03'N	72°58'E	Citomo (Wk)	Alifu Alifu	11	4°00'N	72°57'E
Beyruhuttaa (U)	Gaafu Alifu	19	0°22'N	73°33'E	Clan Alpine (Wk)	Kaafu	9	4°45'N	73°35'E
Beyrumaaddoo (U)	Gaafu Alifu	19	0°48'N	73°13'E	Club Med Farukolufushi (R)	Kaafu	9	4°14'N	73°33'E
Bihurehaa (U)	Gaafu Alifu	19	0°25'N	73°34'E	Club Med Kanifinolhu (R)	Kaafu	9	4°21'N	73°36'E
Biledhdhoo (I)	Faafu	14	3°07'N	72°59'E	Coco Palm (R)	Baa	7	5°03'N	72°53'E
Bileffahi (I)	Shaviyani	4	6°20'N	72°58'E	Cocoa (R)	Kaafu	10	3°55'N	73°28'E
Bileiytheyrahaa (U)	Laamu	18	2°03'N	73°32'E	Corbin (Wk)	Baa	7	4°54'N	72°56'E
Bis Huraa (U)	Shaviyani	4	6°09'N	73°18'E	Crusader (Wk)	Kaafu	9	4°45'N	73°35'E
Biyaadhoo (U)	Kaafu	10	3°56'N	73°27'E	Dalsja (Wk)	Kaafu	9	4°12'N	73°31'E
Biyadoo (R)	Kaafu	10	3°56'N	73°27'E	Daravandhoo (I)	Baa	7	5°09'N	73°08'E
Boaddoo (U)	Gaafu Alifu	19	0°43'N	73°20'E	Dekaanbaa (U)	Gaafu Dhaalu	20	0°23'N	73°02'E
Boahuraa (U)	Meemu	16	2°56'N	73°36'E	Dhaandhoo (I)	Gaafu Alifu	19	0°37'N	73°28'E
Bodehuttaa (U)	Gaafu Dhaalu	20	0°18'N	73°02'E	Dhabidhoo (I)	Laamu	18	2°06'N	73°33'E

PR - Proposed Resort   R - Resort   U - Uninhabited Island   I - Inhabited Island   WK - Wreck   P - Protected Marine Area

ISLAND NAME	ATOLL	MAP #	REFERENCE	ISLAND NAME	ATOLL	MAP #	REFERENCE
Dhakandhoo (U)	Baa	7	5°15'N 72°54'E	Dhoores (U)	Dhaalu	15	2°55'N 72°53'E
Dhandhoo (U)	Baa	7	5°14'N 73°10'E	Dhoragali (U)	Raa	6	5°29'N 73°00'E
Dhangethi (I)	Alifu Dhaalu	12	3°36'N 72°58'E	Dhunikolhu (U)	Baa	7	5°03'N 72°53'E
Dhapparu (U)	Haa Alifu	1	6°55'N 73°14'E	Dhururehaa (U)	Thaa	17	2°10'N 73°01'E
Dhapparu (Wk)	Haa Alifu	1	6°55'N 73°14'E	Dhuvaafaru (U)	Raa	6	5°38'N 73°03'E
Dhapparuhuraa (U)	Haa Alifu	1	6°55'N 73°12'E	Dhuvaafaruhuraa (U)	Raa	6	5°38'N 73°03'E
Dharaboodhoo (I)	Faafu	14	3°04'N 72°56'E	Duras (Wk)	Faafu	14	3°16'N 72°49'E
Dharuma (Wk)	Kaafu	9	4°38'N 73°38'E	Eboodhoo (U)	Alifu Dhaalu	12	3°49'N 72°46'E
Dhebaidhoo (U)	Dhaalu	15	2°48'N 73°02'E	Eboodhoo (U)	Baa	7	5°04'N 72°52'E
Dheburidheythereyvaadhoo(U)	Raa	6	5°24'N 72°59'E	Eboodhoo (U)	Kaafu	10	4°05'N 73°31'E
Dheefuram (U)	Noonu	5	5°53'N 73°19'E	Eboodhoofinolhu (U)	Kaafu	10	4°06'N 73°32'E
Dhehassanu Lonu Bui Huraa(U)	Alifu Dhaalu	12	3°36'N 72°54'E	Eboodhoofushi (U)	Dhaalu	15	2°41'N 72°56'E
Dhekenanfaru (U)	Noonu	5	5°55'N 73°09'E	Ebulufushi (U)	Faafu	14	3°08'N 73°02'E
Dhekunuboduveli (U)	Meemu	16	2°49'N 73°27'E	Edipparufushi (U)	Haa Dhaalu	2	6°18'N 72°38'E
Dhekunuvinagandu (U)	Laamu	18	1°50'N 73°16'E	Ehivakaa (U)	Gaafu Dhaalu	20	0°17'N 73°03'E
Dhelibehuraa (U)	Noonu	5	5°51'N 73°27'E	Ehurah Huraa (U)	Kaafu	10	3°49'N 73°25'E
Dherukerehaa (U)	Gaafu Dhaalu	20	0°15'N 73°07'E	Ekasdhoo (U)	Shaviyani	4	6°04'N 73°17'E
Dhevvadhoo (U)	Gaafu Alifu	19	0°34'N 73°15'E	Ekulhivaru (U)	Noonu	5	5°57'N 73°18'E
Dhevvalaabadhoo (U)	Gaafu Alifu	19	0°36'N 73°19'E	Ekuruffushi (U)	Thaa	17	2°16'N 73°13'E
Dhevvamaagala (U)	Gaafu Alifu	19	0°34'N 73°12'E	Ekurufushi (U)	Raa	6	5°46'N 72°52'E
Dhidhdhoo (I)	Alifu Dhaalu	12	3°29'N 72°53'E	Elaa (U)	Thaa	17	2°10'N 73°05'E
Dhidhdhoo (I)	Haa Alifu	1	6°54'N 73°07'E	Ellaidhoo (R)	Alifu Alifu	11	4°00'N 72°57'E
Dhidhdhoo (U)	Lhaviyani	8	5°23'N 73°23'E	Embudhoo Kandu (P)	Kaafu	10	4°05'N 73°32'E
Dhidhdhoo Finolhu (U)	Alifu Dhaalu	12	3°30'N 72°54'E	Embudu Village (R)	Kaafu	10	4°05'N 73°31'E
Dhiffushi (I)	Kaafu	9	4°27'N 73°43'E	Equator Village (R)	Seenu	21	0°42'S 73°09'E
Dhiffushi (U)	Alifu Dhaalu	12	3°29'N 72°49'E	Erlangen (Wk)	Kaafu	9	4°47'N 73°27'E
Dhiffushi (U)	Lhaviyani	8	5°23'N 73°38'E	Eriyadhoo (U)	Kaafu	9	4°35'N 73°25'E
Dhiffushi (U)	Thaa	17	2°31'N 73°14'E	Eriyadhoo (U)	Shaviyani	4	6°06'N 73°17'E
Dhigali (U)	Raa	6	5°28'N 72°57'E	Eriyadu (R)	Kaafu	9	4°35'N 73°25'E
Dhigali Haa (P)	Baa	7	5°08'N 73°02'E	Erruh-huraa (U)	Meemu	16	3°03'N 73°37'E
Dhiggaru (I)	Meemu	16	3°07'N 73°34'E	Etheremadivaru (U)	Alifu Alifu	11	4°07'N 72°56'E
Dhiggiri (R)	Vaavu	13	3°38'N 73°29'E	Eththigili (U)	Raa	6	5°58'N 72°56'E
Dhiggiri (U)	Alifu Dhaalu	12	3°52'N 72°55'E	Eydhafushi (I)	Baa	7	5°06'N 73°04'E
Dhigihera (U)	Seenu	21	0°41'S 73°08'E	Faadhoo (U)	Lhaviyani	8	5°26'N 73°37'E
Dhigudhoo (U)	Gaafu Alifu	19	0°33'N 73°32'E	Faanahuttaa (U)	Gaafu Dhaalu	20	0°18'N 73°24'E
Dhigufaruhuraa (U)	Haa Alifu	1	6°56'N 72°58'E	Faandhoo (U)	Dhaalu	15	2°58'N 72°57'E
Dhigufaruvinagadu (U)	Baa	7	5°22'N 72°59'E	Faanuvaahuraa (U)	Faafu	14	3°13'N 72°58'E
Dhigufinolhu (R)	Kaafu	10	3°58'N 73°30'E	Faarafushi (U)	Raa	6	5°46'N 72°58'E
Dhigulaabadhoo (U)	Gaafu Dhaalu	20	0°13'N 73°09'E	Fainu (I)	Raa	6	5°28'N 73°02'E
Dhigumaafushi (U)	Gaafu Alifu	19	0°24'N 73°34'E	Fainuaadham Huraa (U)	Lhaviyani	8	5°22'N 73°39'E
Dhigurah (I)	Alifu Dhaalu	12	3°32'N 72°56'E	Falhuge Miyaruvani (P)	Kaafu	9	4°11'N 73°26'E
Dhigurah (U)	Gaafu Alifu	19	0°42'N 73°26'E	Falhumaafushi (U)	Gaafu Alifu	19	0°40'N 73°26'E
Dhigurah (U)	Noonu	5	5°44'N 73°22'E	Falhuverrehaa (U)	Gaafu Alifu	19	0°46'N 73°26'E
Dhigu Rah (U)	Shaviyani	4	6°03'N 73°04'E	Farehulhudhoo (U)	Gaafu Dhaalu	20	0°19'N 73°29'E
Dhigurehaa (U)	Gaafu Dhaalu	20	0°25'N 73°00'E	Faress (I)	Gaafu Dhaalu	20	0°12'N 73°12'E
Dhiguvarufinolhu (U)	Faafu	14	3°15'N 73°02'E	Fares (U)	Baa	7	5°14'N 72°53'E
Dhiguvelidhoo (U)	Shaviyani	4	6°02'N 73°05'E	Faress (U)	Laamu	18	1°48'N 73°18'E
Dhikkuredhdhoo (U)	Raa	6	5°34'N 72°57'E	Faridhoo (I)	Haa Dhaalu	3	6°47'N 73°03'E
Dhinnaafushi (U)	Raa	6	5°36'N 72°50'E	Faruhulhedhdhoo (U)	Gaafu Alifu	19	0°52'N 73°15'E
Dhinnolhufinolhu (U)	Alifu Alifu	11	4°07'N 72°44'E	Faruhulhudhoo (U)	Gaafu Alifu	19	0°52'N 73°16'E
Dhirubaafushi (U)	Lhaviyani	8	5°21'N 73°39'E	Farukolhu (U)	Shaviyani	4	6°12'N 73°18'E
Dhiththudi (U)	Meemu	16	2°46'N 73°26'E	Farukolhufunadhoo (I)	Shaviyani	4	6°08'N 73°18'E
Dhiyadhoo (I)	Gaafu Alifu	19	0°29'N 73°33'E	Farukolhufushi (U)	Kaafu	9	4°14'N 73°33'E
Dhiyamigili (I)	Thaa	17	2°20'N 73°20'E	Farukolhuhuttaa (U)	Gaafu Dhaalu	20	0°12'N 73°14'E
Dhiyanigillaa (U)	Gaafu Dhaalu	20	0°19'N 73°02'E	Farumuli (U)	Noonu	5	5°52'N 73°29'E
Dholhiyadhoo (PR)	Shaviyani	4	5°59'N 73°13'E	Fasmendhoo (U)	Raa	6	5°29'N 72°53'E
Dholhiyadhookudarah (U)	Shaviyani	4	5°59'N 73°13'E	Fathilkedeheragadu (U)	Seenu	21	0°37'S 73°08'E
Dhonaerikadoodhoo (U)	Noonu	5	5°39'N 73°19'E	Feevah (I)	Shaviyani	4	6°21'N 73°13'E
Dhonakulhi (U)	Haa Alifu	1	6°51'N 73°04'E	Fehendhoo (I)	Baa	7	4°53'N 72°58'E
Dhonanfushi (U)	Thaa	17	2°29'N 73°19'E	Fehigili (U)	Lhaviyani	8	5°33'N 73°29'E
Dhoni Mighili (R)	Alifu Alifu	11	3°57'N 72°55'E	Felidhoo (I)	Vaavu	13	3°28'N 73°33'E
Dhonfanu (I)	Baa	7	5°12'N 73°07'E	Felivaru (U)	Lhaviyani	8	5°29'N 73°24'E
Dhonveli Huraa (U)	Shaviyani	4	6°11'N 73°18'E	Felivaru (U)	Noonu	5	5°50'N 73°18'E
Dhon Veli (R)	Kaafu	9	4°19'N 73°36'E	Femunaidhoo (U)	Gaafu Dhaalu	20	0°15'N 73°07'E
Dhoonidhoo (U)	Kaafu	9	4°12'N 73°31'E	Fenboafinolhu (U)	Meemu	16	3°10'N 73°24'E
Dhoonirehaa (U)	Gaafu Dhaalu	20	0°11'N 73°12'E	Fenboahuraa (U)	Haa Dhaalu	2	6°23'N 72°42'E
Dhoonirehaa (U)	Gaafu Dhaalu	20	0°20'N 73°30'E	Fenfuttaa (U)	Gaafu Alifu	19	0°43'N 73°17'E

PR - Proposed Resort   R - Resort   U - Uninhabited Island   I - Inhabited Island   WK - Wreck   P - Protected Marine Area

ISLAND NAME	ATOLL	MAP #	REFERENCE	ISLAND NAME	ATOLL	MAP #	REFERENCE
Fenevenehuttaa (U)	Gaafu Dhaalu	20	0°16′N 73°06′E	Fushivelavaru (U)	Noonu	5	5°50′N 73°12′E
Fenfuraaveli (U)	Meemu	16	2°48′N 73°26′E	Fussfaruhuraa (U)	Vaavu	13	3°35′N 73°19′E
Fenfushi (I)	Alifu Dhaalu	12	3°29′N 72°47′E	Gaadhiffushi (I)	Thaa	17	2°15′N 73°13′E
Fenfushi (U)	Raa	6	5°23′N 72°54′E	Gaadhoo (I)	Laamu	18	1°49′N 73°27′E
Fenfushi (U)	Thaa	17	2°18′N 73°16′E	Gaaerifaru (U)	Lhaviyani	8	5°29′N 73°24′E
Fenmeerufushi (U)	Thaa	17	2°16′N 73°14′E	Gaafaru (I)	Kaafu	9	4°44′N 73°30′E
Fenrehaa (U)	Gaafu Alifu	19	0°25′N 73°34′E	Gaafaru (Wk)	Lhaviyani	8	5°29′N 73°24′E
Fenrehaahuttaa (U)	Gaafu Alifu	19	0°26′N 73°35′E	Gaafushi (U)	Haa Alifu	1	6°52′N 73°04′E
Feridhoo (I)	Alifu Alifu	11	4°03′N 72°43′E	Gaagadufaruhuraa (U)	Baa	7	5°23′N 73°04′E
Fesdhoo (U)	Alifu Alifu	11	4°01′N 72°48′E	Gaagandu (U)	Alifu Alifu	11	4°14′N 72°52′E
Fesdu (R)	Alifu Alifu	11	4°01′N 72°48′E	Gaahuraa (U)	Meemu	16	3°09′N 73°31′E
Fesdu Wreck (Wk)	Alifu Alifu	11	4°00′N 72°47′E	Gaakoshinbi (U)	Shaviyani	4	6°17′N 73°01′E
Feydhoo (I)	Seenu	21	0°41′S 73°08′E	Gaalee (U)	Thaa	17	2°33′N 73°09′E
Feydhoo (I)	Shaviyani	4	6°22′N 73°03′E	Gaamathikulhudhoo (U)	Haa Alifu	1	7°03′N 72°59′E
Feydhoo Finolhu (U)	Kaafu	9	4°13′N 73°29′E	Gaathafushi (U)	Alifu Alifu	11	4°02′N 72°48′E
Fieeali (I)	Faafu	14	3°17′N 72°59′E	Gaathu Giri (P)	Kaafu	9	4°15′N 73°32′E
Fihaalhohi (U)	Kaafu	10	3°53′N 73°22′E	Gaathurehaa (U)	Thaa	17	2°10′N 73°01′E
Fihalhohi (R)	Kaafu	10	3°53′N 73°22′E	Gaaudoodhoo (U)	Raa	6	5°45′N 73°01′E
Filadhoo(U)	Gaafu Dhaalu	20	0°24′N 73°00′E	Gadhdhoo (I)	Gaafu Dhaalu	20	0°17′N 73°28′E
Filaidhoo (U)	Raa	6	5°32′N 72°58′E	Gahe Velagalaa (U)	Gaafu Dhaalu	20	0°22′N 73°19′E
Filitheyo (R)	Faafu	14	3°13′N 73°03′E	Galamadhoo (U)	Gaafu Alifu	19	0°33′N 73°32′E
Filitheyo Kandu (P)	Faafu	14	3°12′N 73°03′E	Gallaidhoo (U)	Shaviyani	4	5°58′N 73°07′E
Filladhoo (I)	Haa Alifu	1	6°53′N 73°14′E	Gallandhoo (U)	Haa Alifu	1	6°57′N 72°59′E
Finey (I)	Haa Dhaalu	3	6°45′N 73°03′E	Gan (I)	Laamu	18	1°55′N 73°33′E
Finolhoss (U)	Baa	7	5°14′N 73°07′E	Gan (U)	Gaafu Dhaalu	20	0°16′N 73°26′E
Finolhu (U)	Alifu Dhaalu	12	3°33′N 72°52′E	Gan (U)	Seenu	21	0°42′S 73°09′E
Firubaidhoo (I)	Shaviyani	4	6°07′N 73°13′E	Gangehi (R)	Alifu Alifu	11	4°13′N 72°46′E
Fish Head (P)	Alifu Alifu	11	3°58′N 72°55′E	Gaathu Giri (P)	Kaafu	9	4°15′N 73°32′E
Fiyoari (I)	Gaafu Dhaalu	20	0°13′N 73°08′E	Gasfinolhu (R)	Kaafu	9	4°22′N 73°38′E
Foakaidhoo (I)	Shaviyani	4	6°19′N 73°09′E	Gasgandufinolhu (U)	Laamu	18	1°57′N 73°33′E
Foammulah (I)	Gnaviyani	21	0°17′S 73°25′E	Gasveli (U)	Meemu	16	2°50′N 73°28′E
Fodhdhipparu (U)	Noonu	5	5°45′N 73°12′E	Gaukedi (U)	Seenu	21	0°39′S 73°06′E
Fodhdhoo (I)	Noonu	5	5°44′N 73°13′E	Gazeeraa (U)	Gaafu Dhaalu	20	0°16′N 73°24′E
Fonaddoo (U)	Thaa	17	2°12′N 73°08′E	Gemanafushi (I)	Gaafu Alifu	19	0°27′N 73°34′E
Fonadhoo (I)	Laamu	18	1°50′N 73°30′E	Gemendhoo (I)	Dhaalu	15	2°48′N 73°02′E
Fonagaadhoo (U)	Laamu	18	2°07′N 73°33′E	Gemendhoo (U)	Baa	7	5°17′N 73°02′E
Fondhoo (U)	Thaa	17	2°21′N 72°59′E	Gemendhoo (U)	Noonu	5	5°47′N 73°21′E
Fondidhaani (U)	Thaa	17	2°18′N 73°17′E	George Reid (Wk)	Haa Dhaalu	2	6°24′N 72°34′E
Fonimagoodhoo (U)	Baa	7	5°15′N 73°10′E	Gesskalhuhera (U)	Seenu	21	0°39′S 73°13′E
Foththeyo-bodufushi (U)	Vaavu	13	3°27′N 73°46′E	Giraavaru (R)	Kaafu	9	4°12′N 73°25′E
Four Seasons (R)	Kaafu	9	4°19′N 73°36′E	Giraavaru (U)	Raa	6	5°36′N 72°52′E
Four Seasons (PR)	Baa	7	5°18′N 73°07′E	Giraavaru Kuda Haa (P)	Kaafu	9	4°13′N 73°25′E
Francois (Wk)	Laamu	18	1°53′N 73°14′E	Girifushi (U)	Kaafu	9	4°19′N 73°35′E
French Privateer (Wk)	Gaafu Alifu	19	0°46′N 73°08′E	Goabilivaadhoo (U)	Noonu	5	5°49′N 73°23′E
French Wreck (Wk)	Alifu Alifu	11	4°25′N 72°55′E	Goidhoo (I)	Baa	7	4°53′N 73°00′E
Fuggiri (U)	Raa	6	5°43′N 72°52′E	Goidhoo (I)	Shaviyani	4	6°26′N 72°56′E
Fukumaru (Wk)	Kaafu	9	4°12′N 73°31′E	Golhaallaa (U)	Gaafu Dhaalu	20	0°19′N 73°29′E
Fulangi (U)	Gaafu Alifu	19	0°41′N 73°12′E	Gongalu Huraa (U)	Meemu	16	2°53′N 73°34′E
Fulhadhoo (I)	Baa	7	4°53′N 72°56′E	Gosi (U)	Gaafu Dhaalu	20	0°31′N 73°09′E
Fulidhoo (I)	Vaavu	13	3°41′N 73°25′E	Govvaafushi (U)	Haa Alifu	1	7°01′N 72°55′E
Full Moon Beach Resort (R)	Kaafu	9	4°15′N 73°33′E	Govvaafushi (U)	Lhaviyani	8	5°22′N 73°39′E
Fun Island (R)	Kaafu	10	3°52′N 73°28′E	Goyyafaru (U)	Raa	6	5°34′N 72°56′E
Funadhoo (U)	Baa	7	5°17′N 73°03′E	Guboshi (U)	Raa	6	5°33′N 72°53′E
Funadhoo (U)	Gaafu Alifu	19	0°34′N 73°32′E	Gulhi (I)	Kaafu	10	3°59′N 73°31′E
Funadhoo (U)	Kaafu	9	4°11′N 73°31′E	Gulhi Falhu (P)	Kaafu	9	4°11′N 73°28′E
Funadhooviligili (U)	Gaafu Alifu	19	0°34′N 73°31′E	Gulhiggaathuhuraa (U)	Kaafu	10	3°58′N 73°31′E
Funamadhua (PR)	Gaafu Alifu	19	0°31′N 73°13′E	Guraidhoo (I)	Kaafu	10	3°54′N 73°28′E
Fukumaru (Wk)	Kaafu	9	4°12′N 73°31′E	Guraidhoo (I)	Thaa	17	2°19′N 73°19′E
Furanafushi (U)	Kaafu	9	4°15′N 73°33′E	Guraidhoo (U)	Laamu	18	1°54′N 73°15′E
Furaveri (U)	Raa	6	5°26′N 72°54′E	Guraidhoo Kandu (P)	Kaafu	10	3°54′N 73°28′E
Fushifaru (U)	Alifu Alifu	11	4°13′N 72°53′E	Haafushi (U)	Meemu	16	2°47′N 73°26′E
Fushi (U)	Laamu	18	2°03′N 73°32′E	Hadahaa (PR)	Gaafu Alifu	19	0°31′N 73°27′E
Fushi (U)	Thaa	17	2°12′N 72°58′E	Hadoolaafushi (U)	Lhaviyani	8	5°23′N 73°39′E
Fushi Kandu (P)	Dhaalu	15	3°00′N 72°55′E	Hagedhoo (U)	Gaafu Alifu	19	0°32′N 73°12′E
Fushifaru (U)	Lhaviyani	8	5°29′N 73°31′E	Hagrandhoo (U)	Gaafu Alifu	19	0°51′N 73°13′E
Fushifaru Kandu (P)	Lhaviyani	8	5°29′N 73°31′E	Haguvillaa (U)	Gaafu Alifu	19	0°42′N 73°16′E
Fushifarurah (U)	Shaviyani	4	6°24′N 72°56′E	Hakuraa Club (R)	Meemu	16	2°51′N 73°32′E

PR - Proposed Resort   R - Resort   U - Uninhabited Island   I - Inhabited Island   WK - Wreck   P - Protected Marine Area

ISLAND NAME	ATOLL	MAP #	REFERENCE	
Hakura Thila (P)	Meemu	16	2°57'N	73°32'E
Hakuraahuraa (U)	Meemu	16	2°51'N	73°32'E
Halaveli (R)	Alifu Alifu	11	4°02'N	72°56'E
Halaveli Wreck (Wk)	Alifu Alifu	11	4°03'N	72°55'E
Hanghghaameedhoo (I)	Alifu Dhaalu	12	3°51'N	72°58'E
Hanhushi (U)	Laamu	18	1°57'N	73°16'E
Hanifaruhuraa (U)	Baa	7	5°11'N	73°09'E
Hanifarurah (U)	Baa	7	5°12'N	73°08'E
Hanimaadhoo (I)	Haa Dhaalu	3	6°45'N	73°10'E
Hankede (U)	Seenu	21	0°39'S	73°06'E
Hankedehajara (U)	Seenu	21	0°39'S	73°07'E
Hans Hass Place (P)	Kaafu	9	4°11'N	73°28'E
Hathifushi (I)	Haa Alifu	1	7°02'N	72°50'E
Hathifushi (U)	Thaa	17	2°17'N	73°16'E
Havoddaa (U)	Gaafu Dhaalu	20	0°33'N	73°06'E
Havodigalaa (U)	Gaafu Dhaalu	20	0°32'N	73°05'E
Hayston (Wk)	Haa Dhaalu	2	6°24'N	72°34'E
Hebadhoo (I)	Noonu	5	5°58'N	73°24'E
Hembadhoo (U)	Kaafu	9	4°29'N	73°24'E
Hembadhoo (Wk)	Kaafu	9	4°29'N	73°24'E
Hedha (U)	Laamu	18	1°50'N	73°17'E
Heenfaru (U)	Alifu Dhaalu	12	3°49'N	72°50'E
Helengeli (R)	Kaafu	9	4°38'N	73°34'E
Heretere (U)	Seenu	21	0°38'S	73°14'E
Hevaahulhudhoo (U)	Gaafu Dhaalu	20	0°18'N	73°02'E
Hibalhidhoo (U)	Baa	7	5°08'N	73°07'E
Hikahera (U)	Seenu	21	0°35'S	73°14'E
Hilton Maldives (R)	Alifu Dhaalu	12	3°37'N	72°43'E
Himendhoo (I)	Alifu Alifu	11	3°55'N	72°45'E
Himithi (U)	Faafu	14	3°16'N	72°49'E
Himmafushi (I)	Kaafu	9	4°19'N	73°34'E
Hinaamaagalaa (U)	Gaafu Alifu	19	0°38'N	73°21'E
Hingaahuraa (U)	Vaavu	13	3°22'N	73°35'E
Hinnavaru (I)	Lhaviyani	8	5°29'N	73°25'E
Hiraveri (U)	Raa	6	5°34'N	72°52'E
Hirifushi (U)	Gaafu Alifu	19	0°33'N	73°21'E
Hirilandhoo (I)	Thaa	17	2°16'N	72°56'E
Hirimaradhoo (I)	Haa Dhaalu	3	6°43'N	73°01'E
Hirinaidhoo (U)	Haa Dhaalu	3	6°42'N	72°57'E
Hiriyaadhoo (U)	Lhaviyani	8	5°25'N	73°38'E
Hiriyafushi (U)	Dhaalu	15	2°43'N	72°59'E
Hiriyanfushi (U)	Thaa	17	2°13'N	73°09'E
Hirubadhoo (U)	Shaviyani	4	6°12'N	73°15'E
Hirundhoo (U)	Baa	7	5°13'N	73°09'E
Hitaadhoo (U)	Baa	7	5°01'N	72°56'E
Hithaadhoo (U)	Gaafu Alifu	19	0°51'N	73°15'E
Hithadhoo (I)	Laamu	18	1°48'N	73°23'E
Hithadhoo (I)	Seenu	21	0°37'S	73°05'E
Hiyafushi (U)	Alifu Dhaalu	12	3°28'N	72°53'E
Hoadedhdhoo (I)	Gaafu Dhaalu	20	0°27'N	73°00'E
Hodaafushi (PR)	Haa Dhaalu	3	6°47'N	73°07'E
Hodaidhoo (I)	Haa Dhaalu	3	6°47'N	73°05'E
Hodelifushi (I)	Thaa	17	2°30'N	73°19'E
Holhudhoo (I)	Noonu	5	5°46'N	73°16'E
Holhumeedhoo (U)	Noonu	5	5°45'N	73°15'E
Holhurahaa (U)	Laamu	18	2°03'N	73°32'E
Holiday Island (R)	Alifu Dhaalu	12	3°29'N	72°49'E
Hoothodeyaa (U)	Gaafu Dhaalu	20	0°13'N	73°11'E
Horubadhoo (U)	Baa	7	5°10'N	73°03'E
HP Reef (P)	Kaafu	9	4°19'N	73°35'E
Hudhufushee Finolhu (U)	Dhaalu	15	2°54'N	72°55'E
Hudhufushi (PR)	Lhaviyani	8	5°22'N	73°39'E
Huivani (U)	Noonu	5	5°54'N	73°19'E
Hukurudhoo (U)	Alifu Dhaalu	12	3°34'N	72°43'E
Hulhedhdhoo (U)	Gaafu Dhaalu	20	0°25'N	73°00'E
Hulhidhoo (U)	Vaavu	13	3°29'N	73°32'E
Hulhimendhoo (U)	Gaafu Alifu	19	0°43'N	73°26'E
Hulhimendhoo (U)	Laamu	18	1°49'N	73°23'E
Hulhiyandhoo (U)	Laamu	18	2°05'N	73°33'E
Hulhiyanfushi (U)	Thaa	17	2°16'N	73°13'E
Hulhudhdhoo (U)	Noonu	5	5°49'N	73°19'E
Hulhudheli (I)	Dhaalu	15	2°52'N	72°51'E
Hulhudhoo (U)	Baa	7	5°04'N	73°02'E
Hulhudhoo (U)	Baa	7	5°17'N	73°02'E
Hulhudhoo (U)	Raa	6	5°44'N	73°01'E
Hulhudhuffaaru (I)	Raa	6	5°46'N	73°01'E
Hulhule (U)	Kaafu	9	4°12'N	73°32'E
Hulhudhoo (I)	Seenu	21	0°36'S	73°14'E
Hulhumalé (U)	Kaafu	A	4°13'N	73°32'E
Hulhuvehi (U)	Dhaalu	15	2°52'N	73°02'E
Hunigondirehaa (U)	Gaafu Dhaalu	20	0°26'N	73°00'E
Huraa (I)	Kaafu	9	4°20'N	73°36'E
Huraa (U)	Haa Alifu	1	6°52'N	72°57'E
Huraa (U)	Haa Dhaalu	3	6°41'N	73°06'E
Hurasdhoo (U)	Alifu Dhaalu	12	3°40'N	72°47'E
Hurasfaruhuraa (U)	Shaviyani	4	6°08'N	73°03'E
Hurasveli (U)	Meemu	16	3°01'N	73°37'E
Huravalhi (U)	Lhaviyani	8	5°31'N	73°27'E
Huruelhi (U)	Alifu Dhaalu	12	3°33'N	72°43'E
Huruvalhi (U)	Raa	6	5°24'N	72°58'E
Huthisdhoo (U)	Laamu	18	1°47'N	73°23'E
Huvadhumaa Vattaru (U)	Noonu	5	5°51'N	73°27'E
Huvafen Fushi (R)	Kaafu	9	4°22'N	73°22'E
Huvahandhoo (U)	Haa Alifu	1	6°57'N	72°54'E
Huvahendhoo (U)	Alifu Dhaalu	12	3°39'N	72°58'E
Huvarafushi (I)	Haa Alifu	1	6°58'N	72°53'E
Idimaa (U)	Gaafu Alifu	19	0°24'N	73°34'E
Ifuru (U)	Raa	6	5°43'N	73°02'E
Iguraidhoo (I)	Raa	6	5°28'N	73°02'E
Iguraidhoo (U)	Noonu	5	5°48'N	73°21'E
Ihavandhoo (I)	Haa Alifu	1	6°57'N	72°56'E
Ihuru (U)	Kaafu	9	4°18'N	73°25'E
Innafinolhu (U)	Haa Alifu	1	7°04'N	72°49'E
Innafinolhu Wreck (WK)	Haa Alifu	1	7°04'N	72°49'E
Innafushi (U)	Alifu Dhaalu	12	3°48'N	72°44'E
Innafushi (U)	Baa	7	4°53'N	72°53'E
Innafushi (U)	Haa Dhaalu	2	6°24'N	72°38'E
Innamaadhoo (I)	Raa	6	5°33'N	73°03'E
Innarehaa (U)	Gaafu Alifu	19	0°23'N	73°33'E
Isdhoo (I)	Laamu	18	2°07'N	73°34'E
Island Hideaway (R)	Haa Alifu	1	6°51'N	73°04'E
Issari (U)	Dhaalu	15	2°43'N	72°59'E
Jinnathugau (U)	Faafu	14	3°12'N	73°00'E
Kaaddoo (U)	Thaa	17	2°17'N	73°15'E
Kaadedhdhoo (U)	Gaafu Dhaalu	20	0°29'N	73°00'E
Kaalhahuttaa (U)	Gaafu Dhaalu	20	0°14'N	73°08'E
Kaalhehuttaa (U)	Gaafu Dhaalu	20	0°11'N	73°13'E
Kaashidhoo (I)	Kaafu	9	4°57'N	73°28'E
Kaashidhoo (U)	Gaafu Dhaalu	20	0°20'N	73°26'E
Kaashihulhudhoo (U)	Gaafu Dhaalu	20	0°24'N	73°00'E
Kabaalifaru (U)	Shaviyani	4	6°07'N	73°15'E
Kadahalagalaa (U)	Gaafu Dhaalu	20	0°14'N	73°13'E
Kaddhoo (U)	Laamu	18	1°51'N	73°32'E
Kadevaarehaa (U)	Gaafu Dhaalu	20	0°26'N	73°00'E
Kadimma (U)	Dhaalu	15	2°44'N	73°01'E
Kadimmahuraa (U)	Noonu	5	5°52'N	73°29'E
Kadoodhoo (I)	Thaa	17	2°19'N	72°55'E
Kadoo (Wk)	Thaa	17	2°29'N	72°55'E
Kadoogadu (U)	Raa	6	5°47'N	72°53'E
Kadufushi (U)	Thaa	17	2°32'N	72°59'E
Kaduhulhudhoo (I)	Gaafu Alifu	19	0°21'N	73°33'E
Kadumoonufushi (U)	Faafu	14	3°18'N	72°54'E
Kaduviligili (U)	Gaafu Alifu	19	0°52'N	73°12'E
Kafathalhaahera (U)	Seenu	21	0°41'S	73°07'E

PR - Proposed Resort   R - Resort   U - Uninhabited Island   I - Inhabited Island   WK - Wreck   P - Protected Marine Area

ISLAND NAME	ATOLL	MAP #	REFERENCE		ISLAND NAME	ATOLL	MAP #	REFERENCE
Kafenaa (U)	Gaafu Dhaalu	20	0°32'N 73°00'E		Kilisfaruhuraa (U)	Shaviyani	4	6°06'N 73°03'E
Kafidhoo (U)	Thaa	17	2°19'N 72°58'E		Kinolhas (I)	Raa	6	5°27'N 73°02'E
Kagi (U)	Kaafu	9	4°41'N 73°30'E		Kiraidhoo (U)	Dhaalu	15	2°47'N 73°02'E
Kaiaidhoo (U)	Noonu	5	5°59'N 73°19'E		Kisserehaa (U)	Gaafu Alifu	19	0°39'N 73°08'E
Kakai-ariyadhoo (U)	Haa Dhaalu	3	6°28'N 72°54'E		Koalaa (U)	Noonu	5	5°51'N 73°29'E
Kakolhas (U)	Thaa	17	2°19'N 72°57'E		Kodaanafuttaa (U)	Gaafu Dhaalu	20	0°20'N 73°30'E
Kalhahadhihuraa (U)	Alifu Dhaalu	12	3°48'N 72°43'E		Kodedhoo (U)	Gaafu Dhaalu	20	0°25'N 73°00'E
Kalhaidhoo (I)	Laamu	18	1°59'N 73°32'E		Kodegalaa (U)	Gaafu Dhaalu	20	0°23'N 73°24'E
Kalhefalaa (U)	Gaafu Dhaalu	20	0°21'N 73°02'E		Kodey (I)	Gaafu Alifu	19	0°30'N 73°33'E
Kalhehigili (U)	Gaafu Dhaalu	20	0°18'N 73°02'E		Kodeymatheelaabadhoo (U)	Gaafu Alifu	19	0°31'N 73°30'E
Kalherehaa (U)	Gaafu Dhaalu	20	0°15'N 73°20'E		Kodeyviligili (U)	Gaafu Alifu	19	0°31'N 73°33'E
Kalhudheyfushi (U)	Thaa	17	2°18'N 73°17'E		Kodghutigalla (U)	Gaafu Dhaalu	20	0°17'N 73°12'E
Kalhufahalafushi (PR)	Thaa	17	2°25'N 73°22'E		Kodufuttaa (U)	Gaafu Alifu	19	0°41'N 73°26'E
Kalhuhuraa (U)	Kaafu	10	4°01'N 73°22'E		Kodurataa (U)	Gaafu Dhaalu	20	0°23'N 73°02'E
Kalhuhuttaa (U)	Gaafu Dhaalu	20	0°20'N 73°02'E		Kolaa (U)	Gaafu Alifu	19	0°50'N 73°11'E
Kalhumanjehuraa (U)	Lhaviyani	8	5°33'N 73°30'E		Kolamaafushi (I)	Gaafu Alifu	19	0°50'N 73°11'E
Kalhuoiyfinolhu (U)	Lhaviyani	8	5°22'N 73°38'E		Kolhufushi (U)	Noonu	5	5°48'N 73°28'E
Kalhuohfummi (Wk)	Meemu	16	2°47'N 73°26'E		Kolhufushi (U)	Thaa	17	2°16'N 73°13'E
Kalhurahaa (U)	Laamu	18	1°51'N 73°16'E		Kolhufushi (U)	Thaa	17	2°22'N 73°22'E
Kaludirehaa (U)	Gaafu Alifu	19	0°26'N 73°34'E		Kolhuvaariyaafushi (I)	Meemu	16	2°46'N 73°26'E
Kamadhoo (I)	Baa	7	5°17'N 73°08'E		Komandhoo (U)	Shaviyani	4	6°03'N 73°04'E
Kanamana (U)	Haa Dhaalu	3	6°43'N 72°54'E		Komandhoo (R)	Lhaviyani	8	5°29'N 73°26'E
Kanandhoo (U)	Gaafu Dhaalu	20	0°16'N 73°04'E		Konottaa (PR)	Gaafu Dhaalu	20	0°28'N 73°09'E
Kandaru (U)	Laamu	18	2°03'N 73°32'E		Kooddoo (U)	Gaafu Alifu	19	0°44'N 73°26'E
Kandaru (U)	Thaa	17	2°19'N 73°19'E		Kothaifaru (U)	Raa	6	5°32'N 72°51'E
Kandhja Ali Madath (Wk)	Kaafu	A	4°11'N 73°31'E		Kottafaru (U)	Raa	6	5°31'N 72°52'E
Kandholhudhoo (I)	Raa	6	5°37'N 72°52'E		Kottefaru (U)	Raa	6	5°31'N 73°03'E
Kandholhudhoo (U)	Alifu Alifu	11	4°00'N 72°53'E		Kuburudhoo (I)	Haa Dhaalu	3	6°39'N 73°02'E
Kanditeem (I)	Shaviyani	4	6°26'N 72°55'E		Kuda Anbaraa (U)	Vaavu	13	3°26'N 73°26'E
Kandooma (R)	Kaafu	10	3°54'N 73°28'E		Kuda Giri (Wk)	Kaafu	10	3°58'N 73°30'E
Kandoomafushi (U)	Kaafu	10	3°54'N 73°28'E		Kuda Huraa (U)	Kaafu	9	4°19'N 73°36'E
Kandu Huraa (U)	Seenu	21	0°37'S 73°09'E		Kuda Kandiheraganda (U)	Seenu	21	0°37'S 73°08'E
Kanduoiygiri (U)	Kaafu	9	4°16'N 73°32'E		Kuda Wataru (U)	Kaafu	9	4°16'N 73°23'E
Kani (U)	Thaa	17	2°12'N 72°58'E		Kudabados (U)	Kaafu	9	4°16'N 73°30'E
Kanifinolhu (U)	Kaafu	9	4°21'N 73°36'E		Kudadhoo (U)	Alifu Dhaalu	12	3°28'N 72°53'E
Kanifushi (U)	Baa	7	5°01'N 72°57'E		Kudadhoo (U)	Baa	7	5°02'N 72°59'E
Kanifushi (U)	Lhaviyani	8	5°22'N 73°20'E		Kudadhoo (U)	Lhaviyani	8	5°30'N 73°27'E
Kanimeedhoo (U)	Thaa	17	2°12'N 73°07'E		Kudadhoo (U)	Shaviyani	4	6°26'N 72°54'E
Kanneiyfaru (U)	Dhaalu	15	2°56'N 73°02'E		Kudadhoo (U)	Thaa	17	2°18'N 72°57'E
Kannigallaa (U)	Gaafu Dhaalu	20	0°27'N 73°00'E		Kudafaress (U)	Laamu	18	1°48'N 73°18'E
Kanuoui Huraa (U)	Kaafu	9	4°19'N 73°36'E		Kudafari (I)	Noonu	5	5°53'N 73°24'E
Kanuhuraa (R)	Lhaviyani	8	5°32'N 73°31'E		Kudafarufasgandu (U)	Haa Dhaalu	3	6°43'N 72°56'E
Kaohera (U)	Seenu	21	0°36'S 73°06'E		Kudafehela (U)	Gaafu Alifu	19	0°26'N 73°34'E
Karibeyru Thila (P)	Alifu Alifu	11	4°06'N 72°57'E		Kudafinolhu (U)	Haa Alifu	1	6°59'N 72°53'E
Karimma (U)	Noonu	5	5°39'N 73°23'E		Kudafinolhu (U)	Kaafu	10	3°52'N 73°28'E
Kashidhoo (U)	Baa	7	5°18'N 72°58'E		Kudafolhudhoo (U)	Alifu Alifu	11	4°11'N 72°46'E
Kattalafushi (U)	Haa Dhaalu	3	6°34'N 72°59'E		Kudafunafaru (U)	Noonu	5	5°53'N 73°23'E
Kedevaahera (U)	Seenu	21	0°34'S 73°13'E		Kudafushi (U)	Laamu	18	1°47'N 73°19'E
Kedhigadu (U)	Dhaalu	15	2°42'N 72°51'E		Kudafushi (U)	Noonu	5	5°43'N 73°25'E
Kedhikulhudhoo (I)	Noonu	5	5°57'N 73°25'E		Kudafushi (U)	Raa	6	5°31'N 72°59'E
Kedhivaru (U)	Noonu	5	5°51'N 73°20'E		Kudafuttaa (U)	Gaafu Alifu	19	0°48'N 73°13'E
Keekimini (U)	Shaviyani	4	6°01'N 73°07'E		Kudahaiykodi (U)	Raa	6	5°36'N 72°59'E
Kekuraalhuveli (U)	Meemu	16	2°51'N 73°32'E		Kudahithi (R)	Kaafu	9	4°25'N 73°23'E
Kelaa (I)	Haa Alifu	1	6°57'N 73°13'E		Kudahuraa (U)	Laamu	18	1°51'N 73°32'E
Kelaa (Wk)	Haa Alifu	1	6°57'N 73°13'E		Kudahuvadhoo (I)	Dhaalu	15	2°40'N 72°54'E
Kendheraa (U)	Gaafu Alifu	19	0°44'N 73°17'E		Kudakaaddoo (U)	Thaa	17	2°17'N 73°16'E
Kendhoo (I)	Baa	7	5°17'N 73°01'E		Kudakalhaidhoo (U)	Laamu	18	1°59'N 73°32'E
Keredhdhoo (U)	Gaafu Dhaalu	20	0°16'N 73°06'E		Kudakibidhoo (U)	Thaa	17	2°10'N 73°04'E
Keremitta (U)	Gaafu Dhaalu	20	0°24'N 73°01'E		Kudakurathu (U)	Raa	6	5°35'N 73°03'E
Keyhuvadhoo (U)	Gaafu Dhaalu	20	0°20'N 73°02'E		Kudalafari (U)	Gaafu Alifu	19	0°54'N 73°21'E
Keylakuna (U)	Haa Dhaalu	3	6°36'N 73°01'E		Kudalhaimendhoo (U)	Shaviyani	4	6°01'N 73°18'E
Keyodhoo (I)	Vaavu	13	3°28'N 73°33'E		Kudalhosgiri (U)	Raa	6	5°36'N 72°55'E
Keyodhoo (I)	Baa	7	5°17'N 72°59'E		Kudamuraidhoo (U)	Haa Dhaalu	3	6°38'N 72°55'E
Kibidhoo (I)	Thaa	17	2°10'N 73°04'E		Kudanaagoashi (U)	Haa Dhaalu	3	6°41'N 72°54'E
Kihaadhoo (I)	Baa	7	5°13'N 73°08'E		Kudarah (R)	Alifu Dhaalu	12	3°34'N 72°55'E
Kihaadhuffaru (R)	Baa	7	5°12'N 73°08'E		Kudarah Thila (P)	Alifu Dhaalu	12	3°34'N 72°55'E
Kihavahhuruvalhi (U)	Baa	7	5°18'N 73°03'E		Kudarikilu (I)	Baa	7	5°18'N 73°04'E

PR - Proposed Resort   R - Resort   U - Uninhabited Island   I - Inhabited Island   WK - Wreck   P - Protected Marine Area

ISLAND NAME	ATOLL	MAP #	REFERENCE		ISLAND NAME	ATOLL	MAP #	REFERENCE	
Kudathulhaadhoo (U)	Raa	6	5°24'N	72°54'E	Maadhiguvaru (U)	Gaafu Alifu	19	0°42'N	73°16'E
Kudausfushi (U)	Meemu	16	2°49'N	73°27'E	Maadhoo (U)	Kaafu	10	3°52'N	73°28'E
Kuddrah (U)	Noonu	5	5°50'N	73°19'E	Maaeboodhoo (I)	Dhaalu	15	2°42'N	72°58'E
Kudhebondeyyaa (U)	Gaafu Alifu	19	0°25'N	73°35'E	Maaehivakaa (U)	Gaafu Dhaalu	20	0°17'N	73°03'E
Kudhehulhedhdhoo (U)	Gaafu Dhaalu	20	0°27'N	73°00'E	Maafahi (I)	Haa Alifu	1	6°50'N	73°09'E
Kudhekelaihuttaa (U)	Gaafu Dhaalu	20	0°13'N	73°11'E	Maafaru (I)	Noonu	5	5°49'N	73°29'E
Kudhelifadhoo (U)	Gaafu Dhaalu	20	0°24'N	73°01'E	Maafaru (U)	Raa	6	5°27'N	72°54'E
Kudhiboli (U)	Vaavu	13	3°38'N	73°22'E	Maafehelaa (U)	Gaafu Alifu	19	0°23'N	73°33'E
Kudi Maa (Wk)	Alifu Dhaalu	12	3°36'N	72°53'E	Maafilaafushi (U)	Lhaviyani	8	5°22'N	73°25'E
Kukulhudhoo (U)	Raa	6	5°28'N	72°52'E	Maafinolhu (U)	Haa Alifu	1	7°00'N	72°52'E
Kukurahaa (U)	Laamu	18	1°52'N	73°16'E	Maafunafaru (U)	Noonu	5	5°52'N	73°22'E
Kulhuduffushi (I)	Haa Dhaalu	3	6°37'N	73°04'E	Maafushi (I)	Kaafu	10	3°57'N	73°29'E
Kumundhoo (I)	Haa Dhaalu	3	6°34'N	73°03'E	Maafushi (U)	Dhaalu	15	2°42'N	72°52'E
Kunahandhoo (I)	Laamu	18	1°47'N	73°22'E	Maafushi (U)	Faafu	14	3°15'N	72°59'E
Kunavashi (U)	Vaavu	13	3°37'N	73°23'E	Maafushivaru (U)	Alifu Dhaalu	12	3°37'N	72°54'E
Kunburudhoo (I)	Alifu Dhaalu	12	3°47'N	72°56'E	Maagaa (U)	Alifu Alifu	11	3°59'N	72°58'E
Kunfunadhoo (U)	Baa	7	5°07'N	73°04'E	Maagalaa (U)	Gaafu Dhaalu	20	0°23'N	73°23'E
Kunnamaloa (U)	Noonu	5	5°55'N	73°09'E	Maagau (U)	Dhaalu	15	2°57'N	72°55'E
Kuradhigandu (U)	Meemu	16	2°46'N	73°23'E	Maagefuttaa (U)	Gaafu Alifu	19	0°51'N	73°11'E
Kurali (U)	Meemu	16	2°47'N	73°22'E	Maagodirehaa (U)	Gaafu Dhaalu	20	0°31'N	73°00'E
Kuramaadhoo (U)	Noonu	5	5°53'N	73°08'E	Maagulhi (U)	Thaa	17	2°32'N	73°11'E
Kuramathi (R)	Alifu Alifu	11	4°16'N	72°59'E	Maahera (U)	Seenu	21	0°36'S	73°06'E
Kurandhuvaru (U)	Thaa	17	2°33'N	73°11'E	Maahuraa (U)	Meemu	16	2°48'N	73°26'E
Kuredhdhoo (U)	Lhaviyani	8	5°33'N	73°28'E	Maakadoodhoo (I)	Shaviyani	4	6°14'N	73°16'E
Kuredhdhoo (U)	Gaafu Alifu	19	0°39'N	73°26'E	Maakalhuveli (U)	Laamu	18	1°47'N	73°20'E
Kuredhifushi (U)	Thaa	17	2°10'N	73°02'E	Maakanaarataa (U)	Gaafu Alifu	19	0°49'N	73°12'E
Kuredhigadu (U)	Kaafu	9	4°15'N	73°33'E	Maakurandhoo (U)	Noonu	5	5°42'N	73°18'E
Kuredhivaru (U)	Noonu	5	5°53'N	73°21'E	Maakurathu (I)	Raa	6	5°37'N	73°03'E
Kuredu (R)	Lhaviyani	8	5°33'N	73°28'E	Maalefaru (U)	Dhaalu	15	2°53'N	73°02'E
Kuredu Express (P)	Lhaviyani	8	5°33'N	73°29'E	Maalefushi (U)	Thaa	17	2°18'N	73°18'E
Kurendhoo (I)	Lhaviyani	8	5°20'N	73°28'E	Maalhaveli (U)	Meemu	16	2°54'N	73°35'E
Kuribi (I)	Haa Dhaalu	3	6°40'N	72°59'E	Maalhendhoo (I)	Noonu	5	5°54'N	73°27'E
Kuroshigiri (U)	Raa	6	5°31'N	72°53'E	Maalhoss (I)	Alifu Alifu	11	3°59'N	72°43'E
Kurumba Village (R)	Kaafu	9	4°13'N	73°31'E	Maalhoss (I)	Baa	7	5°08'N	73°07'E
Lady Christine (Wk)	Kaafu	9	4°46'N	73°23'E	Maamaduvvari (U)	Baa	7	5°01'N	72°56'E
Laguna Beach (R)	Kaafu	10	4°07'N	73°26'E	Maamendhoo (I)	Gaafu Alifu	19	0°43'N	73°26'E
Laihaa (U)	Gaafu Dhaalu	20	0°15'N	73°20'E	Maamendhoo (I)	Laamu	18	1°49'N	73°23'E
Landaa Giraavaru (U)	Baa	7	5°18'N	73°07'E	Maamigili (I)	Alifu Dhaalu	12	3°28'N	72°50'E
Landhoo (I)	Noonu	5	5°53'N	73°28'E	Maamigili (U)	Raa	6	5°39'N	72°53'E
Langon Bank (Wk)	Laamu	18	2°06'N	73°31'E	Maamunagau (U)	Raa	6	5°22'N	72°55'E
Lankanfinolhu (U)	Kaafu	9	4°17'N	73°33'E	Maamunagaufinolhu (U)	Raa	6	5°23'N	72°52'E
Lankanfushi (U)	Kaafu	9	4°18'N	73°33'E	Maamutaa (U)	Gaafu Alifu	19	0°51'N	73°25'E
Lankan Thila (P)	Kaafu	9	4°17'N	73°32'E	Maanaagalaa (U)	Gaafu Alifu	19	0°53'N	73°20'E
Lhaabugali (U)	Raa	6	5°33'N	72°53'E	Maandhoo (U)	Laamu	18	1°52'N	73°32'E
Lhaimagu (I)	Shaviyani	4	6°10'N	73°15'E	Maanenfushi (U)	Raa	6	5°45'N	72°58'E
Lhanbugau (U)	Raa	6	5°44'N	72°55'E	Maarandhoo (I)	Haa Alifu	1	6°52'N	72°59'E
Lhavaddoo (U)	Thaa	17	2°18'N	73°18'E	Maarehaa (U)	Gaafu Alifu	19	0°28'N	73°34'E
Lhazikuraadi (P)	Meemu	16	2°57'N	73°32'E	Maarikilu (U)	Baa	7	5°20'N	72°57'E
Lhohi (I)	Noonu	5	5°49'N	73°23'E	Maashigiri (U)	Raa	6	5°31'N	72°49'E
Lhohi (U)	Dhaalu	15	2°57'N	72°59'E	Maathoda (I)	Gaafu Dhaalu	20	0°12'N	73°11'E
Lhohi (U)	Lhaviyani	8	5°19'N	73°28'E	Maaugoodhoo (I)	Shaviyani	4	6°02'N	73°17'E
Lhohi (U)	Raa	6	5°28'N	72°53'E	Maausfushi (U)	Meemu	16	2°48'N	73°26'E
Lhohifushi (R)	Kaafu	9	4°21'N	73°37'E	Maavaafushi (U)	Lhaviyani	8	5°22'N	73°22'E
Lhosfushi (U)	Kaafu	10	3°54'N	73°28'E	Maavaarulaa (U)	Gaafu Dhaalu	20	0°21'N	73°31'E
Lhossaa (U)	Gaafu Alifu	19	0°49'N	73°12'E	Maavah (I)	Laamu	18	1°53'N	73°14'E
Lhossalafushi (U)	Lhaviyani	8	5°19'N	73°29'E	Maavaidhoo (U)	Haa Dhaalu	3	6°31'N	73°03'E
Liboakandhoo (U)	Raa	6	5°44'N	72°56'E	Maavaruhuraa (U)	Faafu	14	3°11'N	73°03'E
Lily Beach (R)	Alifu Dhaalu	12	3°39'N	72°58'E	Maaveahi (U)	Laamu	18	1°50'N	73°17'E
Lions Head (P)	Kaafu	9	4°11'N	73°26'E	Maavedhdhoo (U)	Gaafu Dhaalu	20	0°18'N	73°29'E
Loafaru (U)	Noonu	5	5°47'N	73°17'E	Maavelavaru (U)	Noonu	5	5°48'N	73°10'E
Lonudhoo (U)	Gaafu Dhaalu	20	0°19'N	73°25'E	Maaya Thila (P)	Alifu Alifu	11	4°05'N	72°52'E
Lonudhoohuttaa (PR)	Gaafu Dhaalu	20	0°18'N	73°25'E	Maayafushi (R)	Alifu Alifu	11	4°04'N	72°53'E
Lundhufushi (U)	Raa	6	5°38'N	72°59'E	Machchafushi (R)	Alifu Dhaalu	12	3°36'N	72°53'E
Maabaidhoo (I)	Laamu	18	2°02'N	73°32'E	Madaveli (I)	Gaafu Dhaalu	20	0°28'N	73°00'E
Maabinhuraa (U)	Lhaviyani	8	5°21'N	73°39'E	Madhiriguraidhoo (U)	Lhaviyani	8	5°28'N	73°34'E
Maaddoo (U)	Baa	7	5°06'N	73°04'E	Madhirivaadhoo (U)	Baa	7	5°16'N	73°09'E
Maadheli (U)	Dhaalu	15	2°53'N	72°50'E	Madidhoo (U)	Shaviyani	4	6°18'N	73°07'E

PR - Proposed Resort   R - Resort   U - Uninhabited Island   I - Inhabited Island   WK - Wreck   P - Protected Marine Area

ISLAND NAME	ATOLL	MAP #	REFERENCE
Madifushi (I)	Meemu	16	3°05'N 73°38'E
Madifushi (I)	Thaa	17	2°22'N 73°21'E
Madihera (U)	Seenu	21	0°42'S 73°11'E
Madikuredhdhoo (U)	Shaviyani	4	6°17'N 73°09'E
Madivaafaru (U)	Raa	6	5°37'N 72°58'E
Madivaru (U)	Kaafu	9	4°30'N 73°22'E
Madivaru (U)	Lhaviyani	8	5°28'N 73°22'E
Madivaru (U)	Alifu Alifu	11	4°16'N 73°01'E
Madivaru (P)	Alifu Dhaalu	12	3°36'N 72°43'E
Madivaru Finolhu (U)	Alifu Alifu	11	4°17'N 73°01'E
Madivaruhuraa (U)	Faafu	14	3°16'N 73°01'E
Madi-Ge (Wk)	Alifu Dhaalu	12	3°37'N 72°47'E
Madoogali (R)	Alifu Alifu	11	4°06'N 72°45'E
Madulu (U)	Haa Alifu	1	7°03'N 72°57'E
Maduvvari (I)	Meemu	16	3°07'N 73°34'E
Maduvvari (I)	Raa	6	5°29'N 72°54'E
Maduvvari (U)	Lhaviyani	8	5°17'N 73°30'E
Magoodhoo (I)	Faafu	14	3°05'N 72°58'E
Magoodhoo (I)	Noonu	5	5°47'N 73°22'E
Magoodhoofinolhu (U)	Faafu	14	3°04'N 72°57'E
Magudhdhuvaa (U)	Gaafu Dhaalu	20	0°17'N 73°21'E
Mahaana Elhi Huraa (U)	Kaafu	10	3°49'N 73°24'E
Mahadhdhoo (U)	Gaafu Alifu	19	0°35'N 73°31'E
Mahakanfushi (U)	Laamu	18	1°58'N 73°33'E
Mahibadhoo (I)	Alifu Dhaalu	12	3°45'N 72°58'E
Mahidhoo (U)	Raa	6	5°34'N 72°57'E
Mahutigalla (U)	Gaafu Dhaalu	20	0°16'N 73°12'E
Maidhoo (U)	Lhaviyani	8	5°24'N 73°39'E
Makunudhoo (I)	Haa Dhaalu	2	6°24'N 72°42'E
Makunudhoo Wreck (WK)	Haa Dhaalu	2	6°24'N 72°42'E
Makunudhoo (U)	Kaafu	9	4°32'N 73°24'E
Makunudhoo Kandu (P)	Kaafu	9	4°34'N 73°23'E
Makunudu (R)	Kaafu	9	4°32'N 73°24'E
Makunueri (U)	Faafu	14	3°16'N 72°56'E
Makunufushi (U)	Kaafu	10	3°55'N 73°28'E
Maldives Hilton (R)	Alifu Dhaalu	12	3°37'N 72°44'E
Maldives Victory (Wk)	Kaafu	9	4°11'N 73°31'E
Malé (I)	Kaafu	9	4°11'N 73°31'E
Mallaarehaa (U)	Gaafu Dhaalu	20	0°30'N 73°00'E
Manadhoo (I)	Noonu	5	5°46'N 73°25'E
Manafaru (U)	Haa Alifu	1	7°00'N 72°57'E
Mandhoo (I)	Alifu Dhaalu	12	3°42'N 72°43'E
Maniyafushi (U)	Kaafu	10	4°03'N 73°24'E
Maradhoo (I)	Seenu	21	0°40'S 73°07'E
Maradhoo-Feydhoo (I)	Seenu	21	0°40'S 73°07'E
Mariyamkoyyerataa (U)	Gaafu Dhaalu	20	0°18'N 73°29'E
Maroshi (I)	Shaviyani	4	6°13'N 73°04'E
Mathaidhoo (U)	Gaafu Dhaalu	20	0°19'N 73°02'E
Matheerah (U)	Haa Alifu	1	7°02'N 72°49'E
Mattidhoo (U)	Gaafu Alifu	19	0°40'N 73°23'E
Mathidhoo (U)	Thaa	17	2°21'N 73°21'E
Mathihuttaa (U)	Gaafu Dhaalu	20	0°16'N 73°21'E
Mathikeranahuttaa (U)	Gaafu Dhaalu	20	0°24'N 73°00'E
Mathikomandoo (U)	Shaviyani	4	6°04'N 73°03'E
Mathivereefinolhu (U)	Alifu Alifu	11	4°11'N 72°45'E
Mathiveri (I)	Alifu Alifu	11	4°12'N 72°44'E
Maththureha (U)	Gaafu Alifu	19	0°22'N 73°33'E
Matu (U)	Gaafu Alifu	19	0°53'N 73°20'E
Mayyaafushi (U)	Lhaviyani	8	5°21'N 73°39'E
Medhadihuraa (U)	Lhaviyani	8	5°33'N 73°31'E
Medhafushi (U)	Haa Alifu	1	7°01'N 72°56'E
Medhafushi (U)	Laamu	18	1°58'N 73°33'E
Medhafushi (U)	Lhaviyani	8	5°22'N 73°26'E
Medhafushi (U)	Noonu	5	5°44'N 73°19'E
Medhafushi (U)	Thaa	17	2°21'N 73°21'E
Medhuburiyaa (U)	Gaafu Alifu	19	0°23'N 73°33'E
Medhufaru (U)	Noonu	5	5°44'N 73°25'E
Medhufinolhu (U)	Baa	7	5°01'N 72°57'E
Medhufinolhu (U)	Kaafu	9	4°31'N 73°22'E
Medhufinolhu (U)	Laamu	18	2°04'N 73°32'E
Medhufushi (U)	Meemu	16	2°53'N 73°34'E
Medhugiri (U)	Vaavu	13	3°23'N 73°29'E
Medhuhuttaa (U)	Gaafu Alifu	19	0°28'N 73°34'E
Medhukuburudhoo (U)	Shaviyani	4	6°12'N 73°02'E
Medhurah (U)	Shaviyani	4	6°02'N 73°04'E
Medhurehaa (U)	Gaafu Alifu	19	0°22'N 73°33'E
Medhuvinagandu (U)	Laamu	18	1°50'N 73°16'E
Medufinolhu (U)	Alifu Dhaalu	12	3°31'N 72°55'E
Meedhaahuraa (U)	Lhaviyani	8	5°22'N 73°24'E
Meedhoo (I)	Seenu	21	0°36'S 73°14'E
Meedhoo (I)	Dhaalu	15	3°00'N 73°01'E
Meedhoo (I)	Raa	6	5°27'N 72°57'E
Meedhuffushi (U)	Dhaalu	15	3°00'N 73°00'E
Meedhupparu (R)	Raa	6	5°27'N 72°59'E
Meehunthibeyhuttaa (U)	Gaafu Dhaalu	20	0°15'N 73°06'E
Meeru (R)	Kaafu	9	4°28'N 73°43'E
Meerufenfushi (U)	Kaafu	9	4°28'N 73°43'E
Melaimu (U)	Gaafu Alifu	19	0°52'N 73°11'E
Mendhoo (U)	Baa	7	5°11'N 72°59'E
Mendhoo (U)	Laamu	18	1°47'N 73°23'E
Menthandhoo (U)	Gaafu Dhaalu	20	0°20'N 73°30'E
Meradhoo (U)	Gaafu Alifu	19	0°35'N 73°06'E
Merengihuttaa (U)	Gaafu Dhaalu	20	0°16'N 73°04'E
Mey-yyafushi (U)	Lhaviyani	8	5°27'N 73°36'E
Meyragillaa (U)	Gaafu Dhaalu	20	0°14'N 73°07'E
Migoodhoo (U)	Shaviyani	4	6°14'N 73°14'E
Miladhoo (U)	Noonu	5	5°48'N 73°22'E
Milaidhoo (U)	Baa	7	5°16'N 73°08'E
Milandhoo (U)	Shaviyani	4	6°17'N 73°15'E
Minaavaru (U)	Noonu	5	5°46'N 73°21'E
Minimasgali (U)	Dhaalu	15	2°45'N 72°53'E
Minimasgali (U)	Faafu	14	3°15'N 73°50'E
Minimessaa (U)	Gaafu Alifu	19	0°33'N 73°08'E
Miriyandhoo (U)	Baa	7	5°04'N 73°02'E
Mirihi (R)	Alifu Dhaalu	12	3°37'N 72°47'E
Miyaru Kandu (P)	Vaavu	13	3°35'N 73°30'E
Moofushi (R)	Alifu Dhaalu	12	3°53'N 72°44'E
Mudhdhoo (U)	Baa	7	5°13'N 73°05'E
Mudhimaahuttaa (U)	Gaafu Dhaalu	20	0°16'N 73°21'E
Muiri (U)	Haa Dhaalu	3	6°39'N 72°56'E
Mulhadhoo (I)	Haa Alifu	1	7°01'N 73°00'E
Muli (I)	Meemu	16	2°55'N 73°35'E
Mulidhoo (U)	Haa Alifu	1	6°51'N 73°01'E
Mulikede (U)	Seenu	21	0°39'S 73°13'E
Mullaafushi (U)	Raa	6	5°32'N 72°54'E
Munandhoo (U)	Gaafu Alifu	19	0°36'N 73°30'E
Mundoo (I)	Laamu	18	2°01'N 73°32'E
Munnafushi (U)	Laamu	18	1°59'N 73°18'E
Muraidhoo (I)	Haa Alifu	1	6°51'N 73°10'E
Muravandhoo (U)	Raa	6	5°37'N 72°57'E
Mushimasmingili (U)	Alifu Alifu	11	3°57'N 72°55'E
Musleiygihuraa (U)	Lhaviyani	8	5°33'N 73°30'E
Muthaafushi (U)	Baa	7	5°05'N 72°53'E
Naainfarufinolhu (U)	Shaviyani	4	6°12'N 73°00'E
Naalaafushi (I)	Meemu	16	2°53'N 73°34'E
Naamuli Wreck (Wk)	Baa	7	4°51'N 72°51'E
Nadallaa (I)	Gaafu Dhaalu	20	0°18'N 73°02'E
Naibukaloabodufushi (U)	Dhaalu	15	2°46'N 73°02'E
Naifaru (I)	Lhaviyani	8	5°27'N 73°22'E
Naivaadhoo (I)	Haa Dhaalu	3	6°45'N 72°56'E
Nakatchafushi (U)	Kaafu	9	4°22'N 73°22'E
Nalaguraidhoo (U)	Alifu Dhaalu	12	3°29'N 72°48'E
Nalandhoo (U)	Shaviyani	4	6°19'N 73°14'E
Naridhoo (U)	Haa Alifu	1	6°54'N 73°08'E

PR - Proposed Resort   R - Resort   U - Uninhabited Island   I - Inhabited Island   WK - Wreck   P - Protected Marine Area

ISLAND NAME	ATOLL	MAP #	REFERENCE	
Narudhoo (I)	Shaviyani	4	6°16'N	73°13'E
Naruribudhoo (U)	Shaviyani	4	6°17'N	73°12'E
Nassimo Thila (P)	Kaafu	9	4°17'N	73°32'E
Nelivarufinolhu (U)	Baa	7	5°07'N	73°05'E
Nellaidhoo (I)	Haa Dhaalu	3	6°43'N	72°57'E
Neykurendhoo (I)	Haa Dhaalu	3	6°33'N	72°59'E
Neyo (U)	Raa	6	5°29'N	73°03'E
Neyo (U)	Shaviyani	4	6°27'N	73°03'E
Nibiligaa (U)	Baa	7	5°11'N	72°57'E
Nicolaos Embricos (Wk)	Gaafu Alifu	19	0°50'N	73°25'E
Nika (R)	Alifu Alifu	11	4°11'N	72°46'E
Nilandhoo (I)	Faafu	14	3°03'N	72°53'E
Nilandhoo (I)	Gaafu Alifu	19	0°38'N	73°27'E
Nolhivaramu (I)	Haa Dhaalu	3	6°40'N	73°05'E
Nolhivaranfaru (I)	Haa Dhaalu	3	6°42'N	73°07'E
Noomaraa (I)	Shaviyani	4	6°26'N	73°04'E
Oceana (Wk)	Haa Alifu	1	7°07'N	72°53'E
Ocean Reef Club (R)	Seenu	21	0°42'S	73°10'E
Odagallaa (U)	Gaafu Alifu	19	0°40'N	73°25'E
Olhahali (U)	Kaafu	9	4°41'N	73°27'E
Olhimuttaa (U)	Gaafu Dhaalu	20	0°21'N	73°02'E
Olhudhiyafushi (U)	Thaa	17	2°17'N	73°15'E
Olhufushi (U)	Thaa	17	2°22'N	72°54'E
Olhufushi Finolhu (U)	Thaa	17	2°22'N	72°54'E
Olhugiri (U)	Baa	7	5°00'N	72°54'E
Olhugiri (U)	Thaa	17	2°30'N	73°16'E
Olhurataa (U)	Gaafu Dhaalu	20	0°19'N	73°02'E
Olhutholhu (U)	Laamu	18	1°48'N	73°21'E
Olhuveli (R)	Kaafu	10	3°51'N	73°28'E
Olhuveli (U)	Dhaalu	15	2°41'N	72°56'E
Olhuveli (PR)	Laamu	18	1°49'N	73°24'E
Olhuvelifushi (I)	Lhaviyani	8	5°17'N	73°36'E
Oligandufinolhu (U)	Kaafu	10	3°49'N	73°25'E
Omadhoo (I)	Alifu Dhaalu	12	3°47'N	72°58'E
Omadhoo (I)	Thaa	17	2°10'N	73°01'E
Ookolhufinolhu (U)	Lhaviyani	8	5°17'N	73°37'E
Orimas Thila (P)	Alifu Alifu	11	3°59'N	72°57'E
Orimasvaru (U)	Noonu	5	5°52'N	73°12'E
Orivaru (U)	Noonu	5	5°48'N	73°18'E
Palm Beach (R)	Lhaviyani	8	5°28'N	73°34'E
Palm Tree Island (R)	Kaafu	10	3°58'N	73°31'E
Paradise (R)	Kaafu	9	4°17'N	73°33'E
Passenger Liner (Wk)	Gaafu Alifu	19	0°46'N	73°26'E
Pearl Island (R)	Raa	6	5°27'N	72°59'E
Persia Merchant (Wk)	Haa Dhaalu	2	6°24'N	72°34'E
Pioneer (Wk)	Vaavu	13	3°21'N	73°35'E
Prazer E Allegria (Wk)	Meemu	16	2°55'N	73°35'E
Raabandhihuraa (U)	Meemu	16	3°06'N	73°23'E
Raafushi (U)	Noonu	5	5°39'N	73°18'E
Raalhulaakolhu (U)	Noonu	5	5°41'N	73°24'E
Raavehrehaa (U)	Gaafu Alifu	19	0°46'N	73°26'E
Radhdhiggaa (U)	Alifu Dhaalu	12	3°46'N	72°47'E
Raggadu (U)	Vaavu	13	3°25'N	73°23'E
Rahadhoo (U)	Gaafu Dhaalu	20	0°31'N	73°00'E
Raiymandhoo (I)	Meemu	16	3°06'N	73°38'E
Raiyruhhuraa (U)	Lhaviyani	8	5°24'N	73°39'E
Rakeedhoo (I)	Vaavu	13	3°19'N	73°28'E
Ralhe Odagallaa (U)	Gaafu Dhaalu	20	0°19'N	73°23'E
Randheli (PR)	Noonu	5	5°42'N	73°21'E
Randi 11 (Wk)	Alifu Dhaalu	12	3°30'N	72°54'E
Rangali (U)	Alifu Dhaalu	12	3°37'N	72°43'E
Rangali Finolhu (U)	Alifu Dhaalu	12	3°37'N	72°44'E
Rannalhi (R)	Kaafu	10	3°54'N	73°22'E
Rannamari (Wk)	Kaafu	9	4°18'N	73°25'E
Ranveli (R)	Alifu Dhaalu	12	3°37'N	72°58'E
Rasdhoo (I)	Alifu Alifu	11	4°16'N	73°00'E
Rasfari (P)	Kaafu	9	4°24'N	73°21'E
Rasfari (U)	Kaafu	9	4°24'N	73°21'E
Rasfushi (U)	Haa Dhaalu	3	6°43'N	72°55'E
Rasgetheemu (I)	Raa	6	5°49'N	73°00'E
Rashukolhuhuraa (U)	Alifu Dhaalu	12	3°31'N	72°55'E
Rasmaadhoo (U)	Raa	6	5°34'N	73°03'E
Rathafandhoo (I)	Gaafu Dhaalu	20	0°15'N	73°06'E
Rayvilla Wreck (Wk)	Meemu	16	2°59'N	73°25'E
Redhdhfuttaa (U)	Gaafu Dhaalu	20	0°20'N	73°30'E
Reethi Beach (R)	Baa	7	5°15'N	73°10'E
Reethi Rah (R)	Kaafu	9	4°31'N	73°22'E
Reindeer (Wk)	Alifu Alifu	11	4°15'N	73°00'E
Ravesteyn (Wk)	Alifu Alifu	11	4°16'N	72°44'E
Rhandi 11 (Wk)	Alifu Dhaalu	12	3°29'N	72°53'E
Ribudhoo (I)	Dhaalu	15	2°56'N	72°54'E
Rihiveli (R)	Kaafu	10	3°49'N	73°24'E
Rihiveli (Wk)	Kaafu	10	3°49'N	73°24'E
Riyaala (Wk)	Gaafu Alifu	19	0°46'N	73°08'E
Rodhuvahrenaa (U)	Gaafu Dhaalu	20	0°18'N	73°28'E
Royal Family (Wk)	Haa Dhaalu	3	6°46'N	72°55'E
Royal Island (R)	Baa	7	5°10'N	73°03'E
Ruffushi (U)	Haa Dhaalu	3	6°46'N	72°56'E
Ruhhurihuraa (U)	Vaavu	13	3°22'N	73°30'E
Ruththibirah (U)	Thaa	17	2°10'N	73°03'E
Savaaheli (U)	Seenu	21	0°41'S	73°07'E
Seedhihuraa (U)	Meemu	16	2°52'N	73°34'E
Seedhihuraa Veligandu (U)	Meemu	16	2°52'N	73°34'E
Selhlhifushi (U)	Lhaviyani	8	5°26'N	73°38'E
Skipjack 11 (Wk)	Lhaviyani	8	5°29'N	73°24'E
Soneva Fushi (R)	Baa	7	5°07'N	73°04'E
Soneva Gili (R)	Kaafu	9	4°18'N	73°33'E
SS Seagull (Wk)	Kaafu	9	4°46'N	73°30'E
Suaroge (U)	Laamu	18	1°55'N	73°15'E
Summer Island (R)	Kaafu	9	4°32'N	73°22'E
Sun Island (R)	Alifu Dhaalu	12	3°29'N	72°48'E
Swiss (Wk)	Kaafu	9	4°38'N	73°38'E
Taj Coral (R)	Kaafu	9	4°29'N	73°24'E
Taj Exotica (R)	Kaafu	10	4°06'N	73°32'E
Thaavathaa (U)	Raa	6	5°29'N	72°59'E
Thanburudhoo (U)	Kaafu	9	4°19'N	73°35'E
Thanburudhoo Thila (P)	Kaafu	9	4°19'N	73°35'E
Thaburudhoo (U)	Noonu	5	5°43'N	73°14'E
Thaburudhuffushi (U)	Noonu	5	5°43'N	73°14'E
Thackaru (U)	Gaafu Alifu	19	0°37'N	73°12'E
Thakandhoo (I)	Haa Alifu	1	6°51'N	72°59'E
Theefaridhoo (U)	Haa Dhaalu	3	6°44'N	73°02'E
Thelehuttaa (I)	Gaafu Dhaalu	20	0°18'N	73°03'E
Theluveligaa (U)	Alifu Dhaalu	12	3°40'N	72°54'E
Theyofulhihuraa (U)	Alifu Dhaalu	12	3°46'N	72°58'E
Thila Fushi (U)	Kaafu	9	4°11'N	73°26'E
Thilabolhufushi (U)	Dhaalu	15	2°45'N	73°02'E
Thiladhoo (U)	Baa	7	5°16'N	73°09'E
Thilamaafushi (U)	Lhaviyani	8	5°16'N	73°35'E
Thimarafushi (I)	Thaa	17	2°12'N	73°09'E
Thinadhoo (I)	Gaafu Dhaalu	20	0°32'N	73°00'E
Thinadhoo (I)	Vaavu	13	3°29'N	73°32'E
Thinadhoomaahuttaa (U)	Gaafu Dhaalu	20	0°33'N	73°00'E
Thinehuttaa (U)	Gaafu Dhaalu	20	0°22'N	73°02'E
Thinhuraa (U)	Dhaalu	15	2°47'N	73°02'E
Thinkolhufushi (U)	Thaa	17	2°21'N	73°21'E
Thinrukurehaa (U)	Gaafu Alifu	19	0°23'N	73°34'E
Thoddoo (I)	Alifu Alifu	11	4°27'N	72°58'E
Tholhendhoo (I)	Noonu	5	5°55'N	73°27'E
Tholhufushi (U)	Alifu Dhaalu	12	3°29'N	72°47'E
Thoshigadukolhu (U)	Noonu	5	5°44'N	73°25'E
Thulhaadhoo (I)	Baa	7	5°02'N	72°51'E
Thulhaagiri (R)	Kaafu	9	4°18'N	73°29'E
Thulusdhoo (I)	Kaafu	9	4°23'N	73°39'E

PR - Proposed Resort   R - Resort   U - Uninhabited Island   I - Inhabited Island   WK - Wreck   P - Protected Marine Area

ISLAND NAME	ATOLL	MAP #	REFERENCE
Thunburi (U)	Laamu	18	2°04'N 73°33'E
Thundudhoshu Finolhu (U)	Laamu	18	2°01'N 73°22'E
Thundufushi (R)	Alifu Dhaalu	12	3°47'N 72°44'E
Thunduhuraa (U)	Vaavu	13	3°21'N 73°31'E
Thuraakunu (I)	Haa Alifu	1	7°06'N 72°54'E
Thuvaru (U)	Meemu	16	2°54'N 73°23'E
Twin Island (R)	Alifu Dhaalu	12	3°37'N 72°54'E
Udhdhoo (U)	Dhaalu	15	2°58'N 72°59'E
Ufulandhoo (U)	Raa	6	5°28'N 72°55'E
Ufulingili (U)	Baa	7	5°01'N 72°58'E
Ufuriyaa (U)	Thaa	17	2°22'N 73°22'E
Ugoofaaru (I)	Raa	6	5°40'N 73°02'E
Ugulifinolhu (U)	Haa Alifu	1	6°58'N 72°54'E
Ugulu (U)	Raa	6	5°42'N 73°02'E
Uhehuttaa (U)	Gaafu Dhaalu	20	0°13'N 73°11'E
Uherehaa (U)	Gaafu Alifu	19	0°24'N 73°34'E
Ukulhas (I)	Alifu Alifu	11	4°13'N 72°52'E
Ukurihuttaa (U)	Gaafu Dhaalu	20	0°14'N 73°07'E
Ulegalaa (U)	Gaafu Dhaalu	20	0°24'N 73°22'E
Uligamu (I)	Haa Alifu	1	7°05'N 72°56'E
Umaana (Wk)	Gaafu Alifu	19	0°50'N 73°25'E
Umarefinolhu (U)	Haa Alifu	1	7°01'N 72°51'E
Undoodhoo (U)	Baa	7	5°17'N 73°03'E
Usfushi (U)	Thaa	17	2°15'N 73°13'E
Utheemu (I)	Haa Alifu	1	6°50'N 73°06'E
Uthuruboduveli (U)	Meemu	16	3°02'N 73°37'E
Uthurumaafaru (U)	Raa	6	5°40'N 72°51'E
Uthuruvinagandu (U)	Laamu	18	1°49'N 73°17'E
Uvadhevifushi (U)	Laamu	18	1°59'N 73°32'E
Vaadhoo (I)	Gaafu Dhaalu	20	0°14'N 73°16'E
Vaadhoo (I)	Raa	6	5°52'N 72°59'E
Vadoo (R)	Kaafu	10	4°08'N 73°28'E
Vaagali (U)	Kaafu	10	3°57'N 73°22'E
Vaanee (I)	Dhaalu	15	2°43'N 73°00'E
Vabbinfaru (U)	Kaafu	9	4°18'N 73°26'E
Vabboahuraa (U)	Kaafu	9	4°19'N 73°36'E
Vadinolhu (U)	Laamu	18	2°01'N 73°22'E
Vaffushi (U)	Raa	6	5°38'N 72°51'E
Vaffushihuraa (U)	Raa	6	5°38'N 72°52'E
Vagaaru (U)	Haa Alifu	1	7°06'N 72°53'E
Vagaru (U)	Shaviyani	4	6°05'N 73°12'E
Vaikaradhoo (I)	Haa Dhaalu	3	6°33'N 72°57'E
Vaikaramuraidhoo (U)	Haa Dhaalu	3	6°33'N 72°54'E
Vaireyaadhuvaa (U)	Gaafu Dhaalu	20	0°17'N 73°20'E
Vakarufalhi (R)	Alifu Dhaalu	12	3°34'N 72°54'E
Vakkaru (U)	Baa	7	5°08'N 72°59'E
Valla (U)	Dhaalu	15	2°43'N 72°53'E
Valla-Ihohi (U)	Dhaalu	15	2°44'N 72°53'E
Vammaafushi (U)	Kaafu	10	3°57'N 73°30'E
Vanbadhi (U)	Thaa	17	2°11'N 72°59'E
Vandhoo (I)	Thaa	17	2°18'N 72°57'E
Vandhoo (U)	Raa	6	5°32'N 73°03'E
Varihuraa (U)	Lhaviyani	8	5°18'N 73°29'E
Vashafaru (I)	Haa Alifu	1	6°54'N 73°09'E
Vashahera (U)	Seenu	21	0°41'S 73°08'E
Vashavarrehaa (U)	Gaafu Dhaalu	20	0°15'N 73°18'E
Vashugiri (U)	Vaavu	13	3°38'N 73°22'E
Vattaru (U)	Noonu	5	5°40'N 73°23'E
Vattaru (U)	Vaavu	13	3°14'N 73°26'E
Vattaru Kandu (P)	Vaavu	13	3°14'N 73°26'E
Vavathi (U)	Noonu	5	5°48'N 73°13'E
Vavvaru (U)	Lhaviyani	8	5°25'N 73°22'E
Velassaru (U)	Kaafu	10	4°07'N 73°26'E
Velavaru (R)	Dhaalu	15	2°59'N 73°01'E
Velidhoo (I)	Noonu	5	5°40'N 73°17'E
Velidhu (R)	Alifu Alifu	11	4°12'N 72°49'E
Velifinolhu (U)	Haa Alifu	1	6°59'N 72°52'E
Veligadu (U)	Lhaviyani	8	5°31'N 73°26'E
Veligadufinolhu (U)	Laamu	18	1°50'N 73°24'E
Veligandu (R)	Alifu Alifu	11	4°18'N 73°02'E
Veligandu (U)	Haa Dhaalu	3	6°45'N 72°56'E
Veligandu Huraa (R)	Kaafu	10	3°58'N 73°31'E
Veraaviligillaa (U)	Gaafu Dhaalu	20	0°19'N 73°27'E
Veriheiybe (U)	Meemu	16	3°02'N 73°37'E
Veymandhoo (I)	Thaa	17	2°11'N 73°06'E
Veyofushi (U)	Baa	7	5°14'N 73°09'E
Veyvah (I)	Meemu	16	2°57'N 73°36'E
Veyvah (U)	Lhaviyani	8	5°26'N 73°22'E
Veyvah (U)	Raa	6	5°46'N 72°54'E
Vicissitude (Wk)	Haa Alifu	1	7°07'N 72°49'E
Vihafarufinolhu (U)	Lhaviyani	8	5°27'N 73°35'E
Vihafarufinolhu (U)	Noonu	5	5°41'N 73°17'E
Vihamaafaru (I)	Alifu Alifu	11	4°07'N 72°44'E
Vihamanaafushi (U)	Kaafu	9	4°13'N 73°31'E
Vilamendhoo (R)	Alifu Dhaalu	12	3°38'N 72°58'E
Viligalaa (U)	Gaafu Alifu	19	0°32'N 73°19'E
Viligili (I)	Gaafu Alifu	19	0°45'N 73°26'E
Villingili (I)	Kaafu	9	4°11'N 73°29'E
Villingili (PR)	Seenu	21	0°41'S 73°12'E
Viligili (U)	Raa	6	5°23'N 72°57'E
Viligilimathidhahuraa (U)	Kaafu	9	4°23'N 73°40'E
Viligilivaru (U)	Alifu Dhaalu	12	3°37'N 72°58'E
Viligilivaru (U)	Kaafu	10	3°55'N 73°27'E
Viligilivarufinolhu (U)	Faafu	14	3°17'N 73°00'E
Villivaru (R)	Kaafu	10	3°55'N 73°27'E
Vilu Reef (R)	Dhaalu	15	3°00'N 73°00'E
Vilufushi (I)	Thaa	17	2°30'N 73°19'E
Vinaneiyfaruhuraa (U)	Baa	7	5°21'N 73°05'E
Voavah (U)	Baa	7	5°19'N 73°04'E
Vodamulaa (U)	Gaafu Alifu	19	0°36'N 73°29'E
Vommuli (U)	Dhaalu	15	2°55'N 72°52'E
Wakkaru (U)	Raa	6	5°29'N 72°57'E
White Sands (R)	Alifu Dhaalu	12	3°30'N 72°54'E
Wooden Wreck (Wk)	Kaafu	9	4°37'N 73°35'E
Ziyaaraiyfushi (U)	Kaafu	9	4°32'N 73°22'E
Ziyaaraiyfushi (U)	Laamu	18	1°59'N 73°18'E

PR - Proposed Resort   R - Resort   U - Uninhabited Island   I - Inhabited Island   WK - Wreck   P - Protected Marine Area